Best TEA SHOP WALKS *in* WEST YORKSHIRE

Norman & June Buckley

Published by Sigma Leisure – an imprint of Sigma Press, 1 South Oak Lane, Wilmslow, Cheshire SK9 6AR, England.

British Library Cataloguing in Publication Data
A CIP record for this book is available from the British Library.

ISBN: 1-85058-708-6

Typesetting and Design by: Sigma Press, Wilmslow, Cheshire.

Cover: from Sandy Gate to Heptonstall *(John Wainwright)*

Maps: Jeremy Semmens

Photographs: the authors

Printed by: MFP Design and Print

Preface

In considering this latest volume in the popular 'Tea Shop Walks' series, the first consideration has to be, what do we mean by 'West Yorkshire'?

Everyone knows about the Yorkshire Dales and the North Yorkshire Moors, but West Yorkshire is less easy to define. It certainly is not the 'West Riding of Yorkshire', the local government administrative area which emerged from medieval boundaries, and which lasted until the reorganisation of 1974. That area was much more extensive, reaching York in the north-east, the Nottinghamshire boundary in the south-east, and included about half of the Yorkshire Dales. Relating 'West Yorkshire' to the southern part of the Pennine Hills is much more relevant, but even now we have to recognise that both Lancashire and Derbyshire lay claim to some of this upland area.

However, if we take the Yorkshire/Lancashire boundary which runs more or less north/south across the high moorland of the Pennines and then move eastwards towards the Leeds/Bradford conurbation, with Skipton and the A59 at the northern end and Holmfirth at the southern end, we have a wide swathe of fine and varied countryside. This area lends itself to eastern extension as far as the Washburn Valley in the north and almost to Barnsley in the south. These extensions allow the inclusion of part of the Wharfe Valley, Swinsty Reservoir and the attractive countryside at Bretton Hall and Cannon Hall. For obvious reasons, the core area of Leeds/Bradford and their satellite towns do not feature in the recommended walks. Despite these urban intrusions, the area has sufficient geographical coherence to be absolutely right for our purpose and the countryside itself could hardly be better for enjoying varied walks and tea shops.

Walks

For those who are unfamiliar with this series of books, the basic format is to combine a circular walk of anything from two to eight miles in length with a recommended tea shop somewhere along the route. The walks tend to be towards the gentle end of the scale but in an area such as West Yorkshire, some fairly tough moorland can be included, adding variety to the river and canal-side paths, the country lanes, the field paths snaking their way across farmland and the stately home parkland which are the staple ingredients. A rich diversity indeed! In practical terms, great care is taken in describing the route; the addition of numbered points, cross referencing with numbers on the relevant sketch plan, should minimise any chance of walkers losing their way. At risk of becoming a total bore to experienced walkers, it should be mentioned that walking boots with semi-rigid soles are recommended for the great majority of these walks and that those which cross moorland may necessitate the use of extra garments, wind and weatherproof.

Designated Trails

Ever since the creation of the Pennine Way a few years after the end of World War II, more and more routes have been formed, largely from stitching together sections of paths already in existence. Some, like the Coast to Coast Path, are entirely valid in providing a link between desirable places. In the case of many others, the motivation is more obscure; however, in all cases the attention focused on the route must help in increasing the use, and probably also the subsequent maintenance, of the various paths involved.

Designated routes used in part in the walks in this book include:

✳ Pennine Way – a few short sections.

✳ Dales Way links – in the Fewston and Ikley Moor areas.

✳ Kirklees Way – in the Shelley/Skelmanthorpe area.

✳ Calderdale Way – a 50-mile circuit looping around the valley of the River Calder – used in the Hebden Bridge/Todmorden areas.

✳ Worth Way – around the valley of the River Worth, Haworth and Oxenhome.

✳ Colne Valley Walk – around the valley of the River Colne, Slaithwaite and Marsen.

✳ Haworth to Hebden Bridge Walk – connects the two small towns.

✳ Station to Station – crosses the moors between railway stations in Yorkshire and Lancashire.

✳ Standedge Trail – around Marsden and the canal and railway tunnels of the same name.

✳ Todmorden Centenary Walk – circles the town on the adjacent hillsides.

✳ Barnsley Boundary Walk – crosses the Bretton Park and Cannon Hall areas.

✳ Dearne Way – crosses Bretton Country Park.

Tea Shops

Similar care is taken in selecting the tea shops. Inevitably, the traditional English variety is well represented but, as always, the opportunity is taken to find and to recommend different types of premises; a canal barge, mining museum canteen, garden centre, stationary railway coach and stately home refectory all contribute to the enhancement of the walks which comes from the enjoyment of good refreshments. Even the traditional tea shop can vary from the Wrinkled Stocking in Holmfirth to Betty's in Ilkley!

Efforts are made to arrange the walk so that the tea shop is placed part way round but in some instances this is not practicable and refreshments must be taken at the end; many walkers may, of course, prefer this format.

Features

To supplement the essential information concerning the route of the walk and its tea shop, any potentially interesting features of the base town or village, plus those encountered along the way, are briefly set out in 'About the Area'.

Format

The speed and ease of use of any type of guide book, particularly walking guides, is a prime consideration. In this and the companion volumes, salient facts are gathered together on the first page of each walk, allowing very quick decisions to be made concerning the suitability of the walk for a person or persons on any particular occasion. The information is presented as:

Length. The distance is chosen rather then the likely time; the author's experience is that a margin as wide as 50% is by no means unusual in timing different walkers over the same route.

Summary. A concise statement about the nature of the walk, any possible difficulties, the length and severity of ascents, the use of public roads, the types of track or footpath and the number of stiles.

Car Parking. Much as one would like walkers to use public transport wherever possible, the reality is that the majority of walkers will reach the start by means of an independent vehicle. Car parking areas are, therefore, recommended in all cases. Wherever possible, car parks requiring payment are avoided, but in some cases this is the only sensible option. Intrusive and environmentally insensitive roadside 'pull offs' are likewise avoided. Concerning public transport, West Yorkshire in general is above average, with particularly good bus route coverage reaching out from the major centres as part of the 'Metro' integrated transport system. The railway services within that system are mentioned where appropriate, but there are far too many bus services to include in a walking guide. Information and timetables are available at the tourist information centres.

Maps

The most useful maps for walkers are the various Ordnance Survey series at the scale of 1:25,000. For many years the green 'Pathfinder' maps, small and relatively expensive, have been the only choice kn most areas. More recently, the 'Outdoor Leisure' (yellow) maps have covered selected areas, usually National Parks and other areas of high landscape quality, in larger, better value, sheets and with some enhancement of the range of information. Some of the sheets in this series have become even better value for money with the introduction of a double sided format. It has to be said that these maps are not designed for people with short arms. The latest development in this map saga is the appearance of the 'Explorer' (orange) series a few years ago, speedily replacing the original Pathfinders in area after area, starting with what appear to be the more attractive visitor destinations. As this book is going to press, this transformation is happening in West Yorkshire.

Contents

The Walks

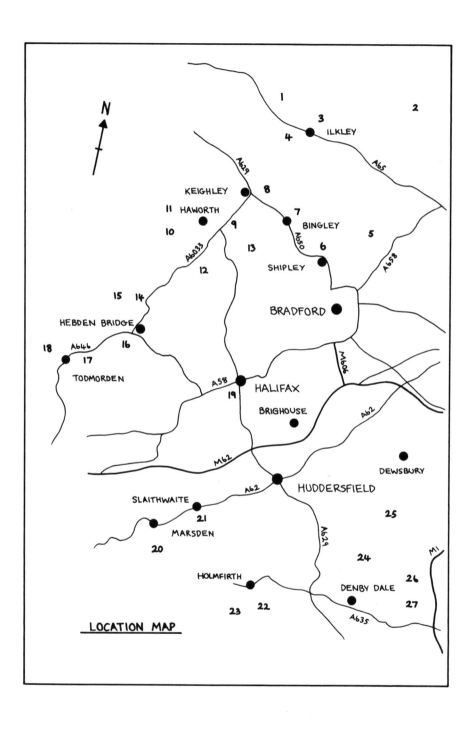

LOCATION MAP

Introduction

The landscape of our area of West Yorkshire is strongly characterised by the Pennine Hills, part of the great chain which stretches from the Edale area of Derbyshire to the Scottish border, and by the rivers, the Worth, the Calder, the Ryburn, the Colne and the Holme, which drain the great upland mass on its east side. All these rivers eventually join the River Aire as it leaves the Yorkshire Dales to wend its way to the south east through the heartland of industrial Yorkshire.

These Pennine Hills are uncompromisingly gritstone, in sharp contrast to the limestone of the Derbyshire Dales to the south and the Yorkshire Dales to the north. Rocky outcrops are minimal and the thin, acid, soil of these high uplands, allied to the harsh climate, has produced a treeless moorland landscape, great heather covered mounds rolling to the horizon, with rough sheep grazing as the only possible agricultural activity.

As the land falls away to the east, enormous deposits of coal underlie the more productive soils that support more diverse farming activities. In the north east of our area, the lower part of the valley of the River Wharfe and the valley of the River Washburn have both escaped the industrial fate of the River Aire and remain as a comparatively gentle, pastoral, landscape.

Human Occupation

Pre-historic

Not surprisingly, evidence of early human occupation of the Pennines is sparse; there was an abundance of much more hospitable land elsewhere for the relatively few 'hunter/gatherer' people; later, as primitive agriculture gradually developed, the river valleys and the lower ground in the east of the area offered a much better existence than the bleak moorland. The Stone, Bronze and Iron Ages have left nothing like the great monuments of more favoured areas such as Wessex, the Cotswolds or the West Country. But, there were people here; there is a Neolithic cairn and a Bronze Age round barrow on Bradley Moor, five miles north west of Keighley, and a whole cluster of Bronze Age monuments on Rombalds (Ilkley) Moor and the adjacent Addingham High Moor, including several stone circles and a large number of 'cup and ring' carvings. The famous 'Swastika Stone' on Rombalds Moor is believed to be from the Iron Age. Whilst most of these relics are in themselves comparatively small scale, collectively they amount to important evidence of prolonged occupation of a relatively small area.

At Almondbury, about two miles south east of Huddersfield, there is a comprehensive Iron Age hillfort, built in four phases over a period of time, the last probably being as recent as the first century BC.

The Romans

In common with most of the north of England, the large and diffuse tribe of the Brigantes occupied what we now call West Yorkshire. The impact on the landscape left by the Romans, after they had subdued the Brigantes, is less than that in many other parts of Britain. Inevitably there were roads, always essential to an occupying power because of the need for speedy movement of forces to concentrate at points of insurrection, where native inhabitants would greatly outnumber sparse local garrisons. Scrutiny of the Ordnance Survey maps will soon reveal that part of the A59 follows a major Roman route across the Pennines, connecting Chester with York. Whilst the lines of the main highways have long been recognised, there are more minor roads of which the route is still by no means certain. This road system opened up large tracts of so far undeveloped ('waste') land, helping the spread of agriculture in later centuries as population growth necessitated migration into areas which, for good reasons, had been regarded as less desirable.

West Yorkshire was probably never a place where wealthy chieftains, Roman or Romano Britsh, built their great villas. If they did, nothing has survived. However, at Ilkley the mineral springs were known and regarded as having medicinal powers. The Roman station here was Olicana; the Manor House stands on this site.

'Dark Ages', Medieval times and later

After the departure of the Romans, constant conflict as waves of Angles, Saxons, Danes and others swept into Yorkshire left the area as one of the under-populated parts of England at the time of the Domesday Book. The population density of about four people to the square mile over the whole of the north of the country was one tenth of that in East Anglia.

As in pre historic and Roman times, West Yorkshire was again a low-key area when the great castles, the abbeys and the priories were built. Although the Wars of the Roses involved much of the area, the relevant castles were at Pontefract, Middleham, Bolton and other locations beyond the area covered by this book. Skipton Castle is probably the nearest. Yorkshire is renowned for the splendour of the abbeys – Fountains, Bolton, Middleham, Jerveaux and the rest – but only Kirkstall Abbey, close to Leeds, is even on the fringe of our area. Similarly, the sheep farming was not sufficiently profitable to result in the construction of great 'wool churches', as in the Cotswolds and most of East Anglia.

A small number of former stately homes, very much at the smaller end of the scale can, however, be found; East Riddlesden Hall, Cannon Hall and Shibden Hall all appear in this book and Oakwell Hall is also within the area.

Medieval and Middle Ages transport was largely by packhorses, using trails established in some number over centuries. Surviving paving and, most of all, packhorse bridges confirm some of these routes and provide most attractive features for today's walkers. West Yorkshire is particularly rich in these bridges, most of them quite delightful; Hebdon Bridge, Haworth, Marsden and Oxenhope all have well known examples.

Industry

Arguably, it was not until the late 18th century and the start of the industrial revolution that West Yorkshire became of place of any importance. Initially, the abundant water supplies, largely in fast flowing Pennine rivers and streams, provided power and process water for the small textile mills, built in large numbers along the valleys to replace the existing cottage industry. Later, the extraction of the coal deposits developed into one of the country's largest and most productive coal fields, covering much of the eastern part of this area. The advent of steam power, hand-in-hand with coal production, led to further centralisation of the textile industry into larger mills. Many of these were no longer limited to the valley bottom sites, but grouped in and around the fast growing towns and cities such as Leeds, Bradford, Huddersfield and Halifax. Possibly the finest surviving example is the huge mill at Saltaire, featured in this book.

Inevitably the rapid growth of such an industry had a dramatic effect on the landscape, not least because of the provision of transport links vital for supplying the mills and for taking away the finished products. Canals, railways and roads, generally in that order, were constructed apace. West Yorkshire soon had a complex network of railway lines criss-crossing the area between coal mines, factories, and the urban centres.

In common with most northern traditional industries, the Yorkshire woollen and other textiles trade has declined. Although mill buildings may be derelict or converted for other use, and many of the railway lines are now disused and in varied stages of dereliction, the visitor can still be in no doubt concerning West Yorkshire's industrial basis. For many people, the surviving evidence of water power enhances a walk; the abandoned weirs, sluices and dams being of interest not only in the sense of history and perhaps working out how it all operated, but sometimes even adding a certain beauty to some stark landscape. Massive, yet graceful, railway viaducts, such as that near Cullingworth, undoubtedly enhance rather than detract from the local scenery. Without these relics, Pennine Yorkshire would be diminished.

Towns and Villages

No one visits this area expecting to find examples of the traditional English village, always assuming that such a village is typified by the biscuit-tin illustration of ancient thatched cottages and inn sitting cosily around a green with spreading horse chestnut trees, all glowing in gentle evening sunshine.

Life is harder here and most of the settlements have an evident 'no nonsense' sense of purpose stemming from the industrial past. That does not, however, mean that they are universally unattractive. Indeed, for many visitors the contrary could be argued. For example, the industrial past of Heptonstall is of the era of the cottage industry, leaving a village by-passed by the industrial revolution, now of immense interest and attraction. Even those small towns, such as Holmfirth, Haworth and Hebden Bridge, in which an early hamlet or series of hamlets had industry superimposed, are still well worth visiting, not least for the added interest of evidence of early industry.

Towards the periphery of the area, particularly towards the York-shire Dales, the industrial impact was much less; Addingham is an example of a relatively unspoilt village.

Literature and the Media

The Brontë family of the 19th century and their home at Haworth comprise by far the most important literary heritage. Just a handful of novels by Charlotte, Emily and Anne have immortalised Haworth and its moors; consciously or otherwise, 'Wuthering Heights' has undoubtedly played a major part in the public perception of the lo-cal landscape and climate.

The late Ted Hughes, Poet Laureate, had strong local connections. He was born at Mytholmroyd, near Hebden Bridge; his wife, Sylvia Plath, celebrated in her own right and as the posthumous subject of a late work by Hughes, is buried in the churchyard at Heptonstall.

To move from the sublime to the (arguably) ridiculous, there are two television creations which rival the Brontës in attracting hordes of visitors to the area. Holmfirth has achieved fame as the heart of the 'Summer Wine Country'. This long-running (since 1971) series of programmes is firmly rooted in the town and the nearby country-side, the settings combining Holmfirth buildings with moorland scenery, much of it close to Marsden.

Although not quite at the same level of visitor popularity, the vil-lage of Esholt forms the core of the 'Emmerdale' soap series, inevita-bly attracting a good number of coach parties and others wanting to see at first hand the inn and other buildings which are featured.

1. Addingham

Summary: A section of the Dales Way by the side of the River Wharfe combines with adjacent higher ground to give an attractive circuit based on the unspoilt village of Addingham. Generally good underfoot but some meadow grass without footpath. Many stiles.

Length: 4¼ miles (6.8km)

Car Parking: Small public car park in Bolton Road, Addingham, 40 metres from the junction of Bolton Road with the village main street. Grid reference 079498.

Maps: Ordnance Survey Explorer 27, Lower Wharfedale and Washburn Valley, 1:25,000. Ordnance Survey Landranger104, Leeds and Bradford, 1:50,000.

The Good Food Shop

The Tea Shop

'The Good Food Shop' can be found on the main street in Addingham – it certainly lives up to its name and is recommended by local residents. Extra to the foods, herbs, and spices sold in the shop, there are café tables where light meals and teas are served – tea by the pot, coffee by the mug or cup, orange juice, lemonade, and other drinks are available. Lunch could be quiche with salad or a choice of sandwiches including poached salmon. For a change try a hot sandwich such as sirloin steak. Home-made scones and cakes always available.

Open: 8am to 4pm Mondays to Fridays and from 8am to 2pm on Saturdays. Tel: 01943 830114

About the Area

Despite the proximity of Bolton Bridge and Bolton Abbey and the southern fringe of the Yorkshire Dales generally, Addingham is one of West Yorkshire's lesser known villages, an attractive place, less obviously post-industrial than the majority of the area. Good stone buildings line the village street, with a variety of shops and inns and a sense of being a real community. The village stands a little way above the River Wharfe, surrounded by hilly country, with stark moorland to the north-east towards Blubberhouses.

One of the great Yorkshire textile entrepreneurs, Samuel Cunliffe Lister, the first Baron Masham, is interred in the family vault at the neat little church, largely renewed in the 18th century. Lister was born in Waterloo year, spending much of his 90-year-long life in mechanical invention, with great financial success despite the odd failure. He purchased three large estates in Yorkshire, including Middleham Castle in the Dales. There is a memorial tablet in marble.

The Walk

Turn right from the car park to walk along Bolton Road. Cross a little bridge over a stream to a footpath which avoids a few metres of road. Pass Addingham Middle School and a junction with Ilkley Road then, in 100 metres, fork right into High Mill Lane to go downhill to a complex that includes the former High Mill.

1. Turn left at the bottom into Olirama Caravan Park, through a gate with a 'Dales Way' waymark. The River Wharfe is close on the right, with the impressive former mill weir. Walk along the caravan site roadway for about 150 metres, then turn right at a 'Dales Way' signpost to follow a narrow footpath by the side of the river. Go through a kissing gate to continue by the river, a lovely route by the tree-fringed water.
    Go over a slightly awkward waymarked stile and, after a short rise, pass a ruined building. There are two more waymarked stiles; at the second descend steeply to the river bank. There are steps and yet another stile. A little further is another stile, then a ladder stile over a high wall, then a rise towards the road, aiming to the right of a substantial property. Go over a waymarked stile on the right and up a few steps to reach the public road.

2. Turn left and then, in 40 metres, turn right to follow the drive to Lobwood House. Stay with the unsurfaced lane as it bends to the left around the back of some farm outbuildings. Pass stables to your left and go between agricultural buildings to head for a walled lane leading to a dismantled former railway overbridge.

3. Note the waymark, go through and turn right, through gates, to take a broad, rough surfaced farm track, rising a little. As this short track ends,

go diagonally left, rising steeply up a large meadow. There is no path on the ground; aim for the top edge of Eller Carr Wood. The views over the Wharfe Valley steadily improve as progress is made. Go over a waymarked stile in a wall, 20 metres above the top edge of the woodland.

4. From this point, according to the Ordnance Survey, the right of way keeps roughly the same line until it intersects another right of way in less than 200 metres, a sharp left turn to join the second right of way then being required. On the ground neither right of way is apparent and a left turn after the stile, to rise steeply by the side of the wall, appears to be a sensible alternative. Forty metres before reaching a wall across the top of the field, turn left over a stile, then right for 50 metres up to a farm track.

   Turn left to enjoy a length of level upland walking, with great views of Wharfedale. Go through a gate and continue, with a wall on the left, to reach a ruined farm, Hag Head Laithe. Go over a stile on the left 10 metres before the buildings and bear right to stay 40 metres or so above a wall on the left, heading for a stile in the wall ahead. The top of a wind turbine is peeping over the hill to the right.

   Cross another meadow, now with a little more wear on the grass, go over another stile and continue the same line across the next meadow. Ahead is Highfield Farm. Head for the corner of a wall, then bear left up the slope, away from the farm. The dam of Chelker Reservoir is visible to the right. Go to a waymarked stile and carry on across the next meadow. The track forks here – two waymarks on an electrical pole.

5. Go through/over the gate/stile on the left to commence the long descent to Addingham, firstly along a narrow field and then through a waymarked gate to pass behind Highfield House. A golf course is soon reached at a gate/stile, with a suitable warning notice. The white posts seem to suggest a route round to the left of the course proper; follow this route until a waymarked stile is reached. Go over, to leave the course by a broad green lane between old hedges, with the ruins of High Laithe Farm to the right and squirrels very apparent. At waymarks on a tree, bear left to stay with the broad lane.

   Go through a waymarked gate and down the edge of a meadow to another little gate/squeezer stile; Addingham is now in view and the path is increasingly evident on the grass. Go through a waymarked gate at the bottom, turning right down an unsurfaced farm access roadway. Reach a public road and turn right.

6. Pass the entrance to Addingham First School, then the Addingham Methodist Chapel, soon reaching the village main street. Turn left to walk to the tea shop in just over 100 metres.

   After tea turn right, pass the public conveniences on the left, and turn into Bolton Road to return to the car park.

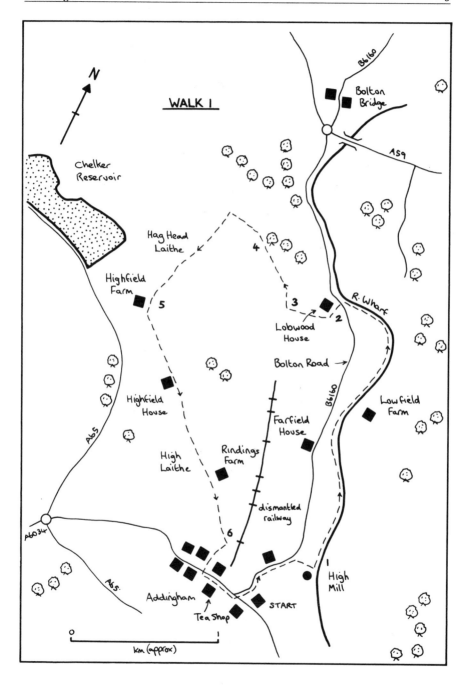

2. Fewston and Swinsty Reservoir

Summary: Probably the easiest walk in the book, in terms of physical effort, in the straightforward nature of the route and in the excellence of the underfoot surfaces. The circumnavigation of Swinsty Reservoir is very attractive; there are no stiles and the wearing of walking boots is not essential.

Length: 3½ miles (5.6km)

Car parking: Well organised free car park, with picnic tables and information board, by the shore of the reservoir. Half a mile south of Fewston village, reached from the A65 by minor roads or by the B6451 and Smithson's Lane. Grid reference 199537.

Maps: Ordnance Survey Explorer 27, Lower Wharfedale and Washburn Valley, 1:25,000. Ordnance Survey Landranger 104, Leeds and Bradford, 1:50,000.

The Tea Shop

Swinsty Tea Garden and Tea Room is rather special. Whilst the outside terrace is sheltered and sun-embracing, the attractive conservatory-style building is elegantly furnished and with fresh flowers from the garden on each table. There is a small self-selection counter; the menu is based on wholefood and vegetarian dishes. Some cooked dishes such as chilli casserole are available. For tea there is a choice of homemade cakes and scones and note that leaf tea, not tea bags, is served here.

The opening hours are restricted but it is well worth planning in advance when to do this delightful walk combined with a visit to an equally delightful tea venue.

Open: 10.30am to 5pm Saturdays, Sundays, and Bank Holidays but closes at 4.30pm outside main season. Also may be closed some weekends in the winter months. Advisable to telephone before visiting. Tel: 01943 880637

About the Area

Separated by high moors from the Lower Wharfe Valley at Ilkley, the

Washburn Valley could be regarded as a little off the beaten track, its bottom long concealed under the extensive waters of the Fewston and Swinsty Reservoirs, satisfying the thirst of Leeds since the 1870s. Thruscross Reservoir, four miles upstream, was added in the 1960s. As is often the case, time, nature and the mellowing of official attitudes have all combined to produce attractive lakes of many of the old municipal reservoirs. The original monotonous regimented tree planting becomes more varied and greater public use is encouraged.

Swinsty and Fewston come well within this category, providing good countryside readily accessible to walkers, with permissive footpaths supplementing the Dales Way link.

Fewston church was rebuilt for the second time in 1697, replacing two previous churches, both destroyed by fire.

The Walk

Walk to the road and turn right, to cross an arm of Swinsty Reservoir on the road causeway. Just before reaching woodland turn right at a waymarked gate signposted 'Dalesway. Haworth to Bolton Abbey Link'

1. Follow a delightful permissive path over close cropped grass, soon entering woodland along a gravelled path. After passing through a gap in a fence, the path becomes more natural. Join a Water Company road, bearing right, pass a 'Leeds Corporation' waterworks building, almost disguised as a chapel, then bear right, past Swinsty Cottage.

2. Cross Swinsty Embankment, the considerable dam at the foot of the reservoir. At the far end of the dam, turn right; there are waymarks at both ends of the dam.

3. The track is now an unsurfaced roadway, separated from the lake shore by a wall and mature conifers. Pass the ancient and fine looking Swinsty Hall to continue along the track, which has become a walled lane bearing left, away from the reservoir, through woodland, mainly conifer with a few beech and oak trees to the right of the lane. This part of the walk is very gently uphill, through Swinsty Nature Reserve. Emerge from the woodland at Swinsty Moor Plantation Car Park, with public conveniences.

4. Turn sharp right to walk down the public road to Fewston Embankment, which separates the two reservoirs. Cross this dam and, as the road bends to the right in front of a house, turn right through an arrangement of fencing – presumably to permit wheelchair access.

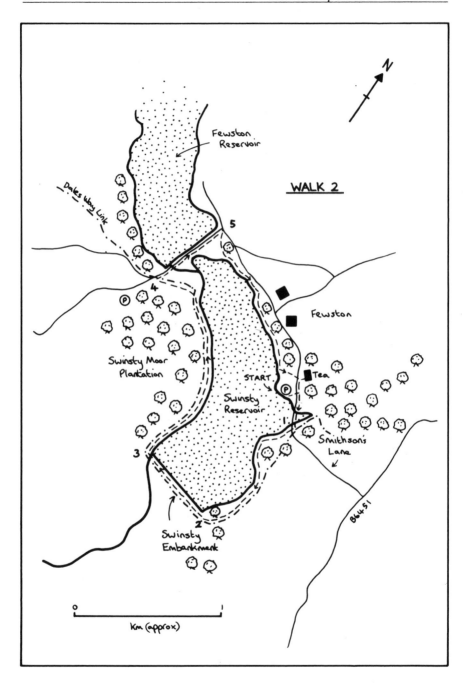

N

Fewston
Reservoir

WALK 2

5

Dales Way Link

Fewston

4

(P)

Swinsty Moor
Plantation

START

(P)

Tea

Swinsty
Reservoir

Smithson's
Lane

3

B6451

2

Swinsty
Embankment

0 _____ 1
Km (approx)

5. Follow another fine permissive Yorkshire Water footpath, initially gravelled and with steps or ramp alternative, soon reaching the shore of the reservoir, then winding alluringly among the trees, arguably the finest part of this entirely pleasant route, all too soon arriving at the waterside picnic area by the car park.

Picnic by Swinsty Reservoir

3. Ilkley and Middleton Woods

Summary: A walk including riverside and woodland paths. Open views from high up the side of Wharfedale across to Ilkley Moor. Generally good paths; less than half a mile of quiet residential road. A modest amount of ascent, at reasonable gradients. Several stiles and plenty of steps, some of which can be greasy.

Length: 3¾ miles (6km)

Car Parking: Roadside car parking for some distance close to the main bridge across River Wharfe. Grid reference 117480.

Maps: Ordnance Survey Explorer 27, Lower Wharfedale and the Washburn Valley, 1:25,000. Ordnance Survey Landranger 104, Leeds and Bradford, 1:50,000.

The Tea Shop

Situated in a side street, 'Muffins' does not have quite the widespread fame of 'Betty's' but it is a good venue for tea and without needing to queue for a table! Service is friendly; decor good with attractive green crockery. Cooked meals are served until 4pm and include sausages with egg and bacon, omelettes, or choices from the blackboard; the filo basket of creamed ham with cheese sounded tempting. Scones, toast, cakes, toasted teacakes are always welcome at tea time.

Open: 9am to 5pm from Monday to Saturday and on Sundays from10.30am to 5pm. Tel: 01943 817505.

About the Area

Below Bolton Bridge, the Wharfe Valley is generally less spectacular than the upper section which reaches past Bolton Abbey to the heart of the Yorkshire Dales. It is, however, still a fine valley, broad enough to accommodate towns such as Ilkley and Otley, but rising steeply to high moorland on either side.

The town of Ilkley claims Roman origins whilst carved stones inside and outside the church of All Saints are believed to be of the 8th and 9th centuries, indicating continuing occupation throughout

Victorian postbox, Ilkley

Saxon times. The church itself is much altered over the years, including a major restoration in the 19th century. A fair amount of 15th century work can be seen and there is a notable 13th century doorway.

As seen today, Ikley is a gracious place with tree lined streets, Victorian shopping arcades and a wealth of tea shops. The railway station is the terminus of a branch line from Leeds.

The Walk

From the town side of the river, cross the road bridge, then turn right in less than 50 metres to descend a ramp to a large grassy public recreation area. The path is close to the river. After passing the rugby club, turn left opposite the corner of a hedge to pass between the rugby ground on the left and open playing fields on the right, heading for an opening in the boundary fence, ahead.

1. Cross a road and head for the swimming pool complex. Pass across the front of the buildings, then bear a little to the left over grass to cross a bridge over a tiny stream then go along a path with steps up to a minor road. Turn left, and then right in 40m at a 'public footpath' sign. Rise to a kissing gate and into Middleton Woods, up another flight of steps. At a signposted junction go left 'public footpath Woodland Walk'.

2. After a length of boardwalk the artificially surfaced path becomes natural, still good and largely under beech and sycamore trees. Cross a plank bridge over a stream and go straight on at the next junction, slightly uphill. Go up more old stone steps, which may be greasy, for a steep little climb up to a fork. Keep right here and continue up more stone steps, reaching another section of the artificially surfaced path. Turn left to proceed to a stile, leaving the wood. Go straight across a meadow to a stile at the top, reaching a minor public road.

3. Turn left along the road and enjoy the gallery-like views over the Wharfe Valley to Ilkley Moor. Join another road, bearing left. Turn right in 30

metres at a 'public footpath' sign into a rough surfaced driveway. To the left are the impressive stone buildings of Myddleton Lodge.

Follow the roadway round to the right, rising a little and passing attractive cottages, in some cases marred by the addition of dormer windows. Bear left immediately before a farm gate, along a track through woodland, with a mixture of conifers, oak and sycamore, undergrown with rhododendron and bramble. Pass an old horse-mounting block and leave the woodland, along an avenue of trees, to reach Tivoli, a fine stone house, on the left at the end of the roadway. Continue along an excellent stony path to join a very minor road.

4. Carry on straight along the road to approach High Austby Cottage, with its well tended garden. Turn left here to go over a stile beside an entrance gateway and commence the descent, over short grass, soon going to the left at a fork, beside tall holly trees. Go through a gate then immediately over a stile and continue straight down the hillside on a well-trodden path through a plantation of young conifers. Go over another stile and, at the bottom of the field, do **not** go over the obvious stile in the wall.

5. Instead, turn sharp left to pass behind the extensive and largely attractive buildings of Low Austby, angling slightly left, uphill, to find a little foot-bridge over a ditch, before going up a few steps to a stile.

Continue along a clear path, initially descending steeply to the bottom of a tiny valley. Go over another stile and round to the right, then cross a meadow above woodland to go to a stile with dog gate. Go over and walk through the woodland of Owler Park on a clear path. Rise to a stile and join a residential roadway close to the Austby gateway.

6. Turn right to continue the descent, passing some fine modern dwellings. At the bottom of Owler Park Road, join another road and turn right. In 20 metres go straight across at a 'T' junction to an obvious footpath, soon reaching the side of the River Wharfe, with some fine willows by the water.

7. Follow this delightful path; there are shingle banks by the water which are ideal for picnics. At a substantial stone bridge turn right to cross the river, then turn left through a gap in a wall and down steps to continue along the far bank, passing public conveniences and the Riverside Hotel, then go along the edge of a large recreation area including a children's playground. At the road bridge go up the steps to return to the parking area. The tea shop is found by walking up New Brook Street to the main part of the town, then turning left.

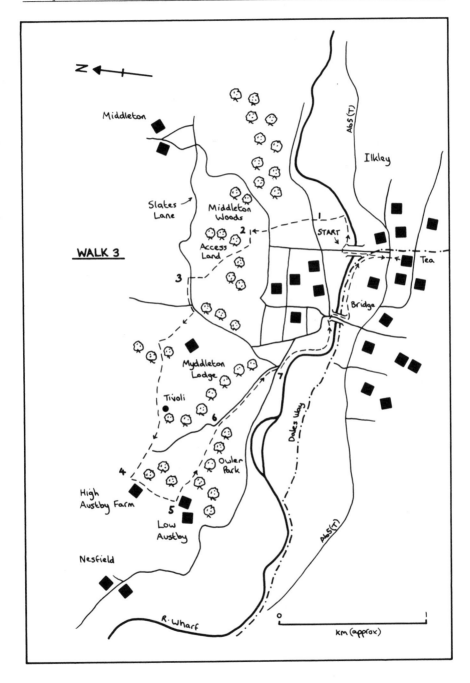

4. Ilkley Moor

Summary: Here it is – inevitably, a substantial walk climbing twice to a high level on the celebrated Ilkley Moor, rather harder than the measured length would indicate. Generally good underfoot, with a few rocky sections, this fine tramp visits the Moor's well known features such as Cow and Calf Rocks, the former bath house at White Wells, Rocky Valley, the Wireless Station, the highest point and the Keighley – Ilkley road over the top. All this plus a visit to the legendary Betty's Tea Shop in Ilkley! No stiles and the only road walking is in Ilkley itself.

Length: 7 miles (11km)

Car Parking: Substantial free car park at Cow and Calf Rocks, with refreshment hut and interpretation boards. Grid reference 133467.

Maps: Ordnance Survey Explorer 27, Lower Wharfedale and Washburn Valley, 1:25,000. Ordnance Survey Landranger 104, Leeds and Bradford, 1:50,000.

The Tea Shop

A Tea Shop Walks book for Yorkshire **must** include a visit to a 'Betty's'. The first of these tea shops opened in Harrogate about eighty years ago. Although founded by a Swiss man, Betty's, with branches in York and other towns, is now a Yorkshire institution; the tea shops attract visitors from all over the world – so do not miss the opportunity and excuse to indulge. The Ilkley 'Betty's' situated in The Grove is a popular venue for both locals and visitors. However, it is not quite the place for wet cagoules and rucksacks and you will probably prefer to de-boot before arrival. The menu is extensive – the traditional high tea of freshly cooked fish and chips served with bread and butter and a pot of tea may prove tempting in spite of the calories; after all, this does follow an energetic few miles! Alternatively, 'the ultimate afternoon tea' may appeal. This comprises sandwiches, scone with butter and jam, plus tea or coffee. Betty's is noted for patisserie; the fruit breads and cinnamon toast are also enjoyable.

Open: 9am to 6pm every day throughout the year but closed on some days during the Christmas/New Year period. Tel: 01943 608029

Betty's café in Ilkley

About the Area

For Ilkley itself, see walk no. 3, Ilkley and Middleton Woods. Like John Peel in the Lake District, the fame of Ilkley Moor is largely due to the popularity of a dire song, in Yorkshire dialect. It is probably incomprehensible in the southern half of the country, with a chorus line of 'On Ilkla Moor baht at' – at least that's how it sounds. The moral of the song, as it continues through innumerable tedious verses, seems to be that a terrible fate awaits those who venture on to the Moor without adequate headwear, presumably necessary to protect oneself from the wild winter (and sometimes wild summer) weather. It is disregarded that the name of the moor as a whole is Rombalds Moor, the true Ilkley Moor being only a small area. But who would want to sing 'On Rombalds Moor baht at'? Somehow it lacks the necessary resonance. Come to think of it the same question could well be asked about singing 'On Ilkla Moor baht at', probably with the same answer! Yet another ironic twist is that on his most recent visit to the moor, scorning the warning in the song, one of the authors of this book set out bareheaded. Eventually, believe it or not, the power of the sun was such that a sun hat had to be donned. Perhaps the originators of the song knew a thing or two after all!

Most of the best features of the moor are towards the northern edge where outcropping rock is at its best at Cow and Calf Rocks and in Rocky Valley. Here also are the greatest concentrations of the evidence of early occupation, notably the 'Cup and Ring' marks and the mysterious 'Swastika Stone'.

The former Roman fort of Olicana is now the site of the Manor House.

From the mid 18th century development of Ilkley as a spa town, a notable survival is at White Wells, up a steep ascent included in this walk. Squire Middleton constructed two open-air spa baths, fed by the adjacent mineral spring, of which the water was so cold that the consequent tingling sensations were believed to have a beneficial effect on the body. These days, many would be more likely to notice other, not necessarily desirable, effects of immersion into chill water hundreds of feet up a bare windswept hillside.

The Walk

Set off steeply uphill on a path reinforced with stone slabs, soon turning left, with Cow and Calf Rocks on the right. On reaching level ground, turn left along a broad track, part of the Dales Way Link long distance path and also the Ebor Way.

1. In less than a quarter of a mile, opposite the Cow and Calf Inn, turn right along another good clear track, soon going steadily uphill, levelling as the plateau of the main part of the moor is reached, ablaze with heather in late summer.

   There are major tracks to right and left here but go straight on along a comparatively minor path through the heather. Continue in much the same direction for about three-quarters of a mile, rising gently, with the route never in doubt. Join a more major track on the right.

2. Bear a little to the left and continue; the masts of the wireless station are visible ahead/right at some distance .

   Join the waymarked Dales Way link beside a small fenced enclosure and turn left, initially over a board walk, rising towards the highest level of the moor, reached at a little cairn close to a prominent upright boundary stone, with initials carved on two faces and a date of 1883.

3. Turn right to follow a level path, weaving its way towards the summit of the moor. Go straight on at a junction, keep left with the major track at a

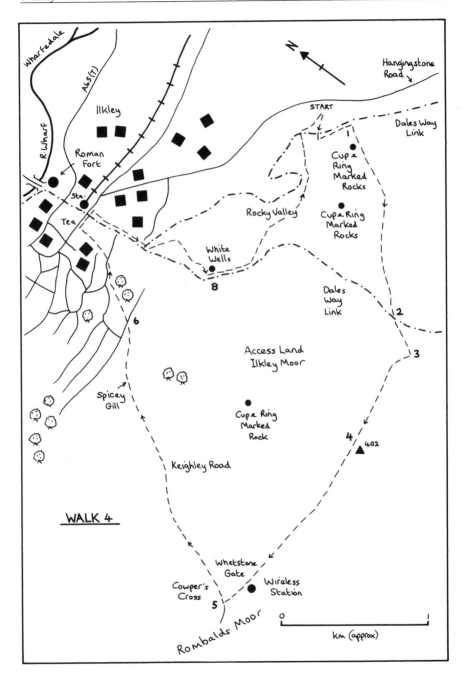

Wharfedale

A65(T)

Ilkley

R. Wharf

Roman Fort

Sta.

Tea

N

START

Hangingstone Road

Dales Way Link

Cup & Ring Marked Rocks

Rocky Valley

Cup & Ring Marked Rocks

White Wells

8

Dales Way Link

2

3

Access Land Ilkley Moor

Cup & Ring Marked Rock

4   402

Spicey Gill

6

Keighley Road

WALK 4

Whetstone Gate

Cowper's Cross

Wireless Station

5

Rombalds Moor

0   1

km (approx)

fork, pass two large rocks which have been prominent for some time, and reach the summit, with cairn and trig point.

4. Carry on towards the wireless station on a similar track, easy enough to follow. Pass a prominent cluster of rocks; one has a bench mark on the far side. There is a wall on the left as the wireless station is approached and a great deal of stone flagged surface and a waymark as an area of peat is crossed. Pass the wireless station to join the old Keighley to Ilkley road, tarmac to the left and a rough surface to the right, without motor vehicles.

5. Turn right to walk towards Ilkley, a fine tramp with the views of and over the town improving progressively, including Middleton Woods and the north side of the Wharfe Valley, included in walk no. 3. On the left is Cowper's Cross, a simple stone monument.

   As the roadway loops away to the left, a short cut path goes straight on, descending more steeply between the bracken and passing a large disused quarry which probably contributed to the considerable growth of Ilkley in the mid-19th century, before rejoining the roadway at the point where a tarmac surface commences. Continue the steep descent, past a delectable picnic spot by a small stream, to join a more important road on the edge of Ilkley town.

6. Cross over and walk down the edge of a small area of amenity land to two old kissing gates. Go through the gate straight ahead, then along the edge of a wooded area with plentiful bramble. Go through another old kissing gate and down a few steps to a residential road, Queens Road. Turn right, passing a large church, turn left down Margarets Terrace, then left down Riddings Road to reach a church with spire at a main shopping street. Betty's Café is across the road, a few metres to the left.

   Start the return by turning left to walk to the main road which runs north/south through the town. Turn right along this road to commence a long uphill slog through an elegant part of Ilkley, by Wells Promenade, with its ribbon of greenery and a little path accompanying a stream in the middle. Cross Queens Road and continue uphill by the roadside, with the moor and the building at White Wells coming into view

   Reach a kissing gate and go up a few steps to follow a 'Dales Way Bradford' sign, passing a children's play area.

7. Pass close to a shelter with a seat then ascend steeply along a well-used track, assisted by what seems like hundreds of steps, to White Wells, where there are picnic tables, poor public conveniences and some refreshments, generally at weekends in season, plus some other busy days. A flag is flown when the place is open. The spring is behind the building.

8. Keep to the right and continue the ascent on a fine wide track, bearing left to head for the striking Ilkley Crags. Before reaching the steps which head for the top of the crags, take a left fork to continue below the crags, with more fine views of Ilkley. Pass through Rocky Valley, the path now rising among the rock scenery. Continue, now downhill, to head straight for the back of the Cow and Calf Rocks.

Ignore any paths to right or left, cross a stream on large rocks, pass a large former quarry on the left, and reach the back of another old quarry set between the main Cow and Calf Rocks, its sheer walls a playground for local rock climbers. Turn right and then bear round to the left for the longer, more gradual descent to the car park.

Turn left, then right, for a shorter, more enterprising route back to your vehicle.

The Cow and Calf Rocks, Ilkley Moor

---

5. Esholt

Summary: A pleasant country walk based on a little village which would hardly be known were it not for the 'Emmerdale' connection. Paths are good throughout, there are few stiles, and the 1¼ miles or so of roadside walking are very quiet. The only significant ascent is along the minor road out of Esholt.

Length: 3¾ miles (6km)

Car Parking: Pay and display car park in Esholt village. Grid reference 182405.

Maps: Ordnance Survey Explorer 27, Lower Wharfedale and Washburn Valley, 1:25,000 (most of the route) Pathfinder 682, Bradford (West Yorks.) (the remainder), 1:25,000. Ordnance Survey Landranger 104, Leeds and Bradford, 1:50,000.

The Tea Shop

Here we are in 'Emmerdale' – for in real life it is the tiny village of Esholt. Ashwood Tea Room, Church Lane, is housed in a converted barn adjacent to the fifteenth century Hall in a picturesque part of the village. The café is packed from floor to ceiling with photographs of the actors and artefacts from the Emmerdale programmes. There are postcards and souvenirs for sale.

Ashwood is open for morning coffee, light lunches, and afternoon teas. Hot and cold drinks, sandwiches freshly made to order, scones, and home-made cakes are always available. Although the café is quite small, there is an outdoor area to have refreshments – if one does not mind providing crumbs for the greedy hens!

Open: 10am to 7pm every day from Easter to October. During the winter months open on Sundays or by prior arrangement. If in any doubt please telephone. Tel: 01274 597866

About the Area

Although situated close to the edge of both the Leeds and the Bradford conurbations, there is surprisingly good countryside at Esholt, particularly to the north. The village has long been a pilgrimage site for those who follow the long running 'soap', 'Emmerdale'. The post office and the tea shop both have a range of souvenir goods for sale. The small church is well situated beyond the Old Hall, which now houses the recommended tea shop.

The village also has St. Leonard's Farm Park, a working family dairy farm with a variety of rare breeds, covered areas, picnic and play areas, nature footpaths, gift shop and refreshments. The site is very child friendly. The Woolpack Inn, in the village centre, features in 'Emmerdale'.

The Tea Shop at Esholt

The Walk

Leave the car park by the entrance roadway and turn right. Go under the railway viaduct and turn right at a road junction to follow Old Hollins Hill, steadily uphill for about half a mile through pleasant countryside, the roadside fringed with bramble, passing a large house in a prominent position by the first bend. As a south thrusting extension of the Guiseley residential area is reached, turn left at a 'public footpath' signpost, over the remains of a stile to follow a grass path between a fence and a wall.

1. Continue to a kissing gate; there are now long views to high ground. Carry on along the edge of a meadow, by a wall. Go over a stile and round to the right, passing a farm.

Cross the main A6038 road to a farm drive, cross a cattle grid and follow the drive, with a wall and a wood to the left. At the top end of the wood, as the drive bends to the left, turn right at a crude 'footpath' sign to walk along the top edge of the meadow, to a stile. Go over and cross a narrow portion of field to a squeezer stile. Go through and turn left along a narrow old walled lane, still rising.

2. To the right is Lane Side Farm. Go through another squeezer stile and continue, now nearing the highest point on the circuit. To the right is a small residential area, obviously an overspill from what appears to be the southern boundary of Guiseley.

    The path continues, a little overgrown in places, by the side of a golf course practice ground. Pass the ninth tee, now slightly downhill, and go through a little wood. At a stile there is a request to follow the footpath marker posts on the golf course, with an 'at your own risk' warning. With suitable caution, carry on, ignoring a waymarked left turn in 70 metres. Go ahead along a farm track, join another track, and descend gently to Lunds Farm, passing a waymark on a post to the right.

3. Pass the farm to continue along an unsurfaced lane, with occasional waymarks on posts. Cross more of the golf course and continue downhill over worn grass, with an outgrown hawthorn hedge on the right. Go along a short length of red shale golf course trolley way; a mill and a railway viaduct are now visible to the left. Keep to the right of a golf teeing area and go down a steep little bank, heading towards a mill pond. Go over a stile in the bottom right corner, turning left over a footbridge.

    Bear left along a driveway to pass the pond, a very attractive place for a picnic, with a cricket ground to the right.

4. Rise towards a war memorial and bear right, through/over a gate/stile and along a wide stony track, initially under trees, into a residential area. On reaching a residential road, turn left at once to descend towards Oak Place on a stony roadway. Fork left before Oak Place and continue downhill past a terrace of cottages and a converted chapel, then into woodland.

    Go right at a 'T' junction, with a mill and its chimney to the left. A surfaced road now leads towards an angled junction with the main road but, in less than 100 metres before this junction, turn left down a flight of steps.

5. Cross the road, bearing slightly right to a well-used track along the edge of a field, with a golf driving range on the left.

    Join a minor road and turn left to head directly towards Esholt village. Cross a stream on a bridge, pass the cricket club, and walk beside the River Aire for part of the total distance of about three-quarters of a mile. In the village, turn right at Church Lane to find the tea shop.

    After tea, return to the road junction, turning right then left to pass the Woolpack Inn and St. Leonard's Farm Park en route to the car park.

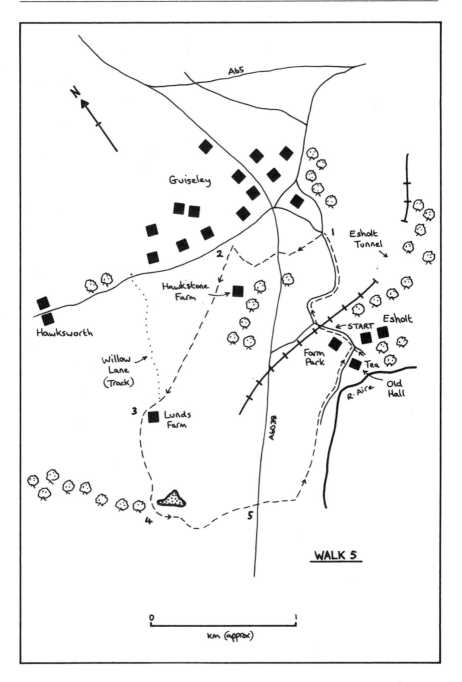

WALK 5

6. Saltaire and Shipley Glen

Summary: A walk full of interest, closer to the Bradford/Shipley built-up area than might be expected from the mainly rural landscape. Titus Salt's mill and model village, the Leeds and Liverpool Canal, Shipley Glen and the adjacent expanse of upland 'common' are all included, as is the Shipley Glen tramway, possibly taking the strain off the rise back to the car park. Paths are all good, mostly very good, with just one section which could slippery when wet. No stiles. A small amount of residential road.

Length: 4¼ miles (6.8km)

Car Parking: There are several informal car parking areas by the side of the common access land, reached by the minor road to the Bracken Hall Countryside Centre, Glen Road. Typical grid reference, 129394.

Maps: Ordnance Survey Pathfinder 682, Bradford (West Yorks.), 1:25,000 – the great majority. Pathfinder 671, Keighley and Ilkley or Explorer 27, Lower Wharfedale and Washburn Valley – a tiny part at the northern end of the route. Ordnance Survey Landranger 104, Leeds and Bradford, 1:50,000.

The Tea Shop

After examining numerous possibilities in Saltaire, our recommendation is Salts Diner, in the mill. It is on the second floor but there is a lift. The decor is interesting, as one might expect in a David Hockney environment; the furniture modern and multi-coloured – rather like a grown-up version of play-group tables and chairs! The choice of food and drink is so comprehensive – we leave it to you! This is a café well worth visiting. Following refreshments it is good idea to walk down through the store – each floor of this enormous building has beautiful furniture, prints, pictures, and many unusual items for the home displayed in spacious surroundings.

Open: 10am to 6pm every day throughout the year except some days in the Christmas/New Year period. Note that hot dishes are not available after 4.30pm. Tel: 01274 530533

About the Area

Saltaire is a remarkable place, a model village built between 1851 and 1876 to house and to provide for all the needs of the employees of the huge textile mill built in 1853 by Titus Salt, who left Bradford to transfer his manufacturing to this new 'green field' site. Salt was one of the great industrial philanthropists of his era, his new village including neat stone cottages, alms houses, shops, institute, wash houses, hospital, railway station, church and a park. There were no pubs, no pawn shops and no police station.

Saltaire is now a conservation area, thriving as a visitor centre, largely unchanged since Salt's day. The mill houses retail businesses, catering and the 1853 David Hockney Gallery, which has the world's largest collection of the work of the Bradford born painter. The unusual United Reformed Church (like most of the great 19th century industrialists, Salt was non conformist), has a striking porch with circular colonnade. Salt died in 1876 and is interred in the mausoleum. Victoria Hall, in Victoria Road, houses the Museum of Victorian Reed Organs and Harmonium.

Salt's Mill at Saltaire

Shipley Glen is another great visitor attraction, the scenery of the glen and adjacent common being supplemented by a discreetly sited fun fair. At one edge of the common, Bracken Hall Countryside Centre has a local countryside exhibition. Shipley Glen Tramway of 1895 claims to be Britain's oldest surviving cable tramway.

Back in Saltaire, the Leeds and Liverpool Canal, dealt with more fully in walk no. 7, Bingley, has a Metro waterbus service running between Shipley and Bingley. The Metro rail service has trains on the line connecting Leeds and Skipton, where there are connections to Lancaster/Morecambe and to Settle and Carlisle.

The Walk

Leave the car parking area by heading north along the path which stays close to Glen Road for a considerable distance, soon passing Bracken Hall. Stay parallel with the road as the common land narrows and the path is progressively nearer to Shipley Glen, the steep-sided, well-wooded, valley to the left. There are some rocky outcrops to be found at the top of the valley side and the views to the higher ground to the right and the open country ahead are better than might be expected so close to a conurbation.

As the wall on the far side of the road turns sharp right, fork left along a good path, passing between concrete posts and bending to the left to descend into the Glen.

1. Cross the stream on a bridge with huge parapets then turn sharp left along a minor path, the lower of two such paths, which rises just a little. The path soon becomes wider, keeping a steady course some way above Loadpit Beck.

    Join another path in about 50 metres and turn left, winding through attractive woodland, silver birch, oak and beech, soon with a wall on the right hand. Continue for some distance to reach the gable ends of a few bungalows of temporary construction.

2. Look out for a minor path on the left, opposite the last bungalow, and descend the valley side, quite steeply in places, to a dam retaining what appears to be a former mill pond

    Cross over the stream and, after passing the end of iron railings, bear right, uphill, on a broad track. At a diagonal crossing of paths go right, more or less on the level, to pass through an area of holly and reach an old walled lane. Turn right in 50 metres at a junction to follow another walled lane, descending gently.

3. Cross a residential road, pass a bus turning circle, and go along Bowland Avenue. Cross another residential road to head for a metal footbridge

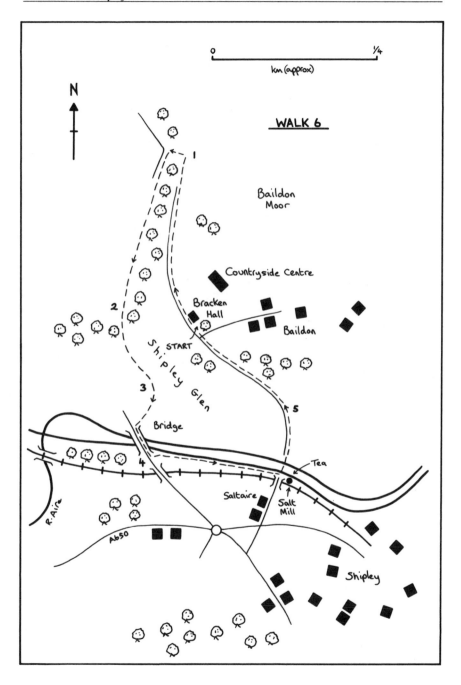

N

WALK 6

km (approx)

Baildon Moor

Countryside Centre

Bracken Hall

Baildon

START

Shipley Glen

Bridge

Tea

Saltaire

Salt Mill

R. Aire

A650

Shipley

over the River Aire. Cross the bridge and continue for a few metres to the Leeds and Liverpool Canal, up a few steps to the towpath.

4. Turn left to walk towards the mill at Saltaire. Leave the canal at the road bridge adjacent to the mill. Turn right along the road for a few metres, and then go to the left to descend the steps to the mill entrance. The lift to the upper floors, including the catering, is at the far end of the ground floor gallery.

After refreshment, leave the mill and turn right, passing the church. Cross the canal on the road bridge. At the bottom of the road turn left, pass the Boathouse Inn, then turn half right at a sign for 'Shipley Glen, the Shipley Glen Tramway and Bracken Hall Countryside Centre'. Cross a metal bridge over the River Aire and then pass through the end of Roberts Park to reach a public road at another signpost.

Cross over, turn left for 100 metres, and then turn right at a third signpost. A tarmac path leads to the bottom end of the tramway.

5. Either use the tramway to return towards Shipley Glen or walk up the adjacent bridleway through the edge of woodland, at a steady gradient. The top tramway terminus is soon reached. Continue along Prod Lane, a quiet residential cul de sac. There may or may not be an accurate signpost just above the tramway terminus. Pass the fun fare site on the left, then the Old Glen House Inn and the public conveniences to reach the open expanse of the common land. Follow any convenient path back to the car parking area.

7. Bingley and Micklethwaite

Summary: A surprisingly good and varied shortish walk using a length of the towpath of the Leeds and Liverpool Canal, then footpaths to visit East Morton and Micklethwaite. The return path weaves ingeniously through residential areas. Apart from a steep section of public road, not hilly and with few stiles, although two are awkward.

Length: 3½ miles (5.6km)

Car Parking: Informal parking area by side of canal, reached by turning to the east off the A650, Keighley to Bradford road 250 metres to the north of Crossflats railway station. Grid reference 104404.

Maps: Ordnance Survey Explorer 27, Lower Wharfedale and the Washburn Valley, 1:25,000 (90% of route). Ordnance Survey Pathfinder 682, Bradford, West Yorks, 1:25,000 (10% of route) Ordnance Survey Landranger 104, Leeds and Bradford, 1:50,000.

The Tea Shop

The canal in Bingley is full of interest; Five Rise Locks Café is situated, as the name suggests, by the flight of locks – in good weather one could spend hours here just watching the boats locking through and mooring nearby to visit the café. The building was originally a staging stable for the exchange of animals when the barges were tugged by horses. The decor is in character with the surroundings – flagged floor and pine furniture. Attractive outside seating overlooks the canal. Very pleasant service here – orders taken at the counter and brought to the table. Savouries include soup with crusty bread, toasted sandwiches, pate with toast. And then the sweets – homemade parkin, carrot cake, fruit cake, addictive gateaux from the display – the apple, custard and caramel pie is wonderful. Tea and coffee are good quality and the 'Five Rise Sundae' is a concoction of three flavours of ice cream with nuts, fruit, and cream.

Open: 10.30am to 5pm Tuesdays to Sundays during high season but also open on Bank Holiday Mondays. Winter months open only on Saturdays and Sundays. Closed for two weeks in December and two weeks in February. You are welcome to telephone to check opening if in any doubt. Tel: 01274 562221.

About the Area

Although overall a fairly nondescript industrial town straggling along the bottom of the Aire Valley, Bingley does have some attractive and quite historic corners worth seeking out, notably the town hall and public parks. More prominent is the unfortunate headquarters of the Bingley Building Society. There are plenty of shops and a station on the railway line from Leeds and Bradford to Keighley and Skipton.

Very much involved in this walk, the Leeds and Liverpool Canal traverses the Aire Valley through Bingley, climbing via two sets of locks to the long level pound which takes it beyond Skipton. This wide canal, (locks 11' 4") 127 miles in length, has for many years been the only operational trans-pennine waterway. Conceived in 1770, it was not until 1816 that through traffic was possible. In addition to being a most attractive cruising waterway, the canal towpath,

included in this walk and in walk no. 8, is much used and esteemed by walkers. The 'Bingley Five Rise' is the most famous set of locks on the whole canal, a fine engineering feature still working on a daily basis.

East Morton is a large village with shops and inns, mostly off the line of this walk but well worth a short diversion. Micklethwaite is an altogether quieter place with no road of any significance, noted for groups of attractive stone buildings by the wayside.

The 'Bingley Five Rise'

The Walk

Walk up the ramp to the canal towpath and turn sharp left to proceed for rather more than half a mile, passing Micklethwaite Wharf and a swing bridge carrying a minor road. There are plenty of moored boats and a boat club adjacent to the starting point. On reaching a minor road at Lingcroft Wharf, turn right to leave the canal, crossing Morton Bridge.

1. In 20 metres go through a gap in the wall on the right of the road and down a few steps to take a footpath, initially tarmac surfaced and fenced on each side. Rise fairly steeply up shallow stone steps, then more steps up to a stile over a wall, rather awkward with a large stone slab.

Continue along a clear path across a sloping meadow, rising towards East Morton village, reached over a stile giving access to a public road.

2. At the first road junction, the main part of the village is to the left. *A diversion here is required to visit the church, post office or other shops.*

From the junction, our return route continues to the right, passing attractive old properties. Look out for a waymarked post on the left 20 metres after passing the highest point on the road and turn right as indicated by the post.

3. Pass through a narrow opening and down steps to descend to the side of Morton Beck. Cross the substantial Hebble Bridge then go uphill along an old walled lane, lined with elder and bramble, to reach Peas Acre, an outlying part of Micklethwaite.

Join a public road by a Methodist Chapel.

4 Turn right to walk down the village street, with many good properties and a Victorian post box to admire. As the road bends to the left, and the best of Micklethwaite has been passed, turn left about 40 metres after the bend into Thornfield Mews to walk towards a row of cottages. As the road bends left, leave the tarmac to walk over paving setts.

Turn right at the cottages to a gate/stile at the end, then take a track angling up across the meadow to a stile near the top end of a short wall. Go over and continue along the top edge of a meadow to an awkward 'stile' made of iron bars in the top left corner. After this, turn left, uphill, along the edge of a field to a stile giving access to a narrow lane, between walls. Turn right for a pleasant short walk to a public road.

5. Turn left at the road, Greenhill Lane, steeply uphill for about 300 metres, passing Greenhill Farm and some modern residential development. At the top there is a junction with the more major Lady Lane. Go through a little gate on the right with a 'public footpath' sign and down steps to commence the long descent back to the canal. A well-used path threads its

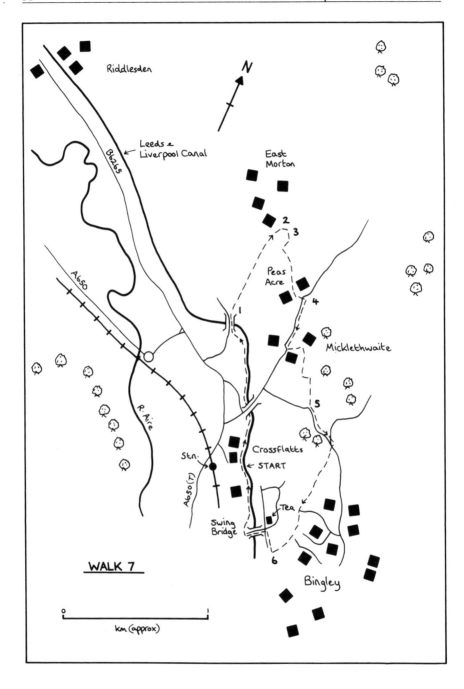

Riddlesden

Leeds &
Liverpool Canal

B6265

A650

East
Morton

2
3

Peas
Acre

1

4

Micklethwaite

R. Aire

A650(T)

Stn.

5

Crossflatts

← START

Swing
Bridge

Tea

6

Bingley

WALK 7

0   1
km (approx)

way through an extensive residential suburb of Bingley, the path surroundings being well wooded and with a surprisingly rural ambience. Reach a residential road, cross over to Pinedale, and continue along this remarkable path. Cross a surfaced driveway; the path continues through a gap in a wall and down a few steps. Go through an old kissing gate on to a surfaced roadway, soon reaching a public road at a 'T' junction.

6. Turn right for 200 metres to a mini roundabout, then turn left for 50 metres to reach the canal. The tea shop, with fine canal-side situation, is immediately on the right.

After refreshments, return to the swing bridge by the top of the celebrated Bingley Five Rise locks, cross and turn right to stroll along the towpath for about a quarter of a mile back to the car parking area.

8. Riddlesden and East Riddlesden Hall

Summary: This modest walk combines a length of the towpath of the Leeds and Liverpool Canal with footpaths across agricultural land along the east side of Airedale, with good views across the valley. There is only a moderate amount of ascent, none of it steep, but there are plenty of stiles, one or two of them being awkward. Generally good paths and three quarters of a mile of quiet roadside walking.

Length: 4¼ miles (6.8km)

Car Parking: Informal space for up to three vehicles by the entrance to the former Isolation Hospital, reached along Hospital Road after turning right at the Marquis of Granby Inn, on the minor road opposite the entrance to East Riddlesden Hall. Grid reference 084424. Alternatively, there is layby space near Moorside Farm, Ilkley Road. Grid reference, 086432.

Maps: Ordnance Survey Explorer 27, Lower Wharfedale and Washburn Valley, 1:25,000. Ordnance Survey Landranger 104, Leeds and Bradford, 1:50,000.

The Tea Shop

The tea room at this National Trust property can be accessed without paying admission or needing to produce a membership card. However, a visit to East Riddlesden Hall is certainly recommended. Tea rooms at National Trust properties have a reliable reputation but this must rank as one of the very best.

Lunches are available – soup with wholemeal bread, salads with roast ham or turkey, or try the Yorkshire cheese platter. For tea there are excellent cakes such as coffee or chocolate sponge or the fruit cake served with Wensleydale cheese. Beverages include Yorkshire tea (said to suit the water) coffee, hot chocolate; cold drinks offered include elderflower cordial. This tea room is especially kind to children; there is a special menu, unbreakable plates and dishes in an attractive pattern, bottle warming service, and even a box of toys – all very thoughtful.

The furniture is pleasing; attractive blue and white patterned crockery; pleasant and efficient waitress service, all contribute to an enjoyable visit, but watch-out for the low beams in this lovely converted barn.

Open: 12pm to 4.30pm from 1ˢᵗ April (or Easter if earlier) to 1ˢᵗ November each day except Thursdays and Fridays (open on Good Friday and on Thursdays in July and August). Also open some days during the Christmas period. Tel: 01535 607075

About the Area

Although situated on the far side of the broad valley of the River Aire, Riddlesden is to all intents and purposes a large outlying residential suburb of Keighley. Not the prettiest place in West Yorkshire, Keighley is, nevertheless, not without interest, with a lively shopping centre and visitor attractions such as Cliffe Castle, a Victorian mansion which is now a museum displaying the story of Airedale past and present, local natural history and minerals.

The preserved Keighley and Worth Valley steam railway is another major attraction, with its terminus station adjoining the main

East Riddlesden Hall

line station and a railway centre at nearby Ingrow. The railway is more fully described in walk no. 9, Haworth and the Worth Valley. Keighley has rail services on the lines connecting Leeds and Bradford with Skipton, Lancaster and Morecambe, Settle and Carlisle. There is also a busy bus station.

East Riddlesden Hall is perhaps one of the National Trust's lesser known properties; it is, however quite a little gem, an ancient house remodelled in the 1600s by a merchant, James Murgatroyd of Halifax. Inside, a wonderful collection of Yorkshire oak furniture, pewter and delicate needlework and embroideries can be seen. The pretty grounds contain a magnificent 17thcentury oak framed great barn and a large pond and are used for many events during a long season from March to December. The shop and tea room are accessible without having to pay for admission to the Hall, which is open during the afternoon (not Fridays, or Thursdays except in July and August) throughout the normal National Trust season from late March to the end of October.

The Leeds and Liverpool Canal stays fairly close to the River Aire on its route from Skipton to Leeds. It is described more fully in walk no. 7, Bingley.

The Walk

From the parking area by the old hospital entrance set off along the signposted narrow path, separated from the hospital grounds by a wall; walkers in shorts—beware the nettles! In less than 200 metres look out for a squeezer stile on the left. Go through and follow a just visible path over grass up the left-hand side of a meadow, rising steadily, soon bearing right to walk alongside How Beck. As height is gained, the first of the long views is apparent. Go up to a gate/stile at the top and continue to rise along a green cart track, with West Morton coming into view. At a junction by farm gates turn right to cross a solidly constructed bridge and walk towards the farm buildings of West Morton.

1.   At the near corner of a converted barn turn left through a little stile to walk past the gable of the building, go over a waymarked stile, then another waymarked stile in 40 metres.

Keep to the edge of a meadow, with a wall close on the right. Ahead is an obvious gate; ignore this and make for a high, awkward stile in the top left corner. Go over and head for the marked steps in front of a row of cottages. Go to the left to pass round the cottages and steeply up to a very minor road.

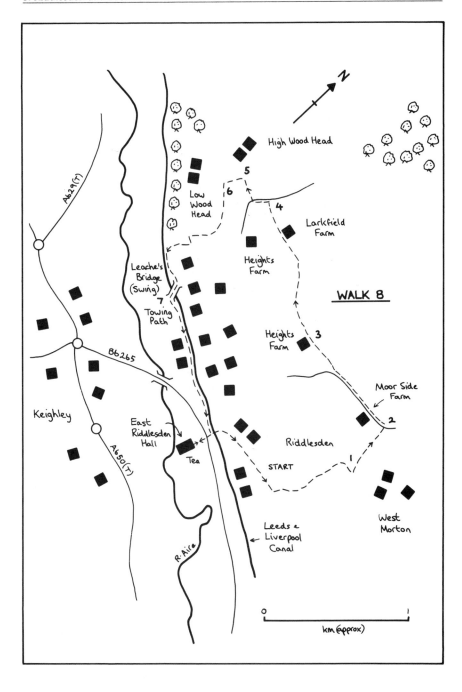

2. Turn left to follow the road for about 500 metres, enjoying even better views than before. As the road dips and bears to the left, go straight ahead to a gate/stile and walk behind a substantial dwelling, then along a green lane between walls. Heights Farm is ahead. Go through a squeezer stile, then right at once to another stile, then left along the bottom edge of a meadow. Pass between agricultural buildings, with a gate, and bear right on a stony track. Go through a gate to head for a farm complex — 'The Height'. Go through a gate, right then left at the farmyard.

3. On leaving the farm turn left through a gap in a fence immediately after a Nissen type building and make for a little iron gate to head for Larkfield Farm. Pass the farmhouse over a cobbled surface, then a barn conversion and continue along a surfaced roadway beneath an avenue of trees to reach the public road.

4. Turn left, downhill, pass Crown House and, as the road bends left, turn right into a stony lane leading to High Wood Head, soon passing a private drive dipping towards a house on the left. In less than 100 metres turn left along a little footpath - there is a rather obscure 'nature trail' notice on the right of the main track at this junction.

5. Descend for a few metres, cross the private drive and go over a stile in the wall opposite. Bear left to head for a squeezer stile and follow the obvious path across a field to Low Wood Head. Go over a stile with a makeshift little gate, into the garden of Low Wood House, pass the end of the house and go through a gate to reach the surfaced access drive.

6. Follow this across the hillside. On reaching trees turn right, through a little gate with a 'nature trail 10' marking, to descend a clear path along the edge of the meadow to a little gate in the bottom corner. Go down a few steps to a roadway. Go straight across to a gravelled track lined with bramble, soon reaching a tarmac road, bearing left. Just before reaching houses, turn right, downhill, into woodland, along a good path. At a little cluster of houses turn left along the access drive.

   The canal is now beside us; turn right to cross a swing bridge, Leache's Bridge.

7. Turn left to walk along the towpath, passing a large canalside former warehouse, a swing bridge carrying a road, another former warehouse and Bar Lane Visitor moorings.

   At the next swing bridge turn right, to go down a minor road to traffic lights. Cross the main road to walk straight to East Riddlesden Hall.

   After refreshments/visit to the Hall, return to the swing bridge and turn right, into Hospital Road, by the Marquis of Granby Inn for a steady, uphill, plod back to the parking place.

9. Haworth and the Worth Valley

Summary: This walk makes a good introduction to Haworth and the Worth Valley, with a dash of moorland to add variety. Part of the walk is through agricultural landscape and one or two of the paths are a little rough. There are several stiles and some ascents, most notably on roadsides within Haworth itself.

Length: 4 miles (6.4km)

Car Parking: Parking for about a dozen vehicles by the roadside of the B6144, Haworth to Cullingworth road about half a mile east of, and well above, Haworth railway station. Grid reference 042371.

Maps: Ordnance Survey Outdoor Leisure 21, South Pennines, 1:25,000. Ordnance Survey Landranger 104, Leeds and Bradford, 1:50,000.

The Tea Shop

There are plenty of tea shops in Haworth. Our chosen venue for much needed tea was Emma's Eating Parlour. Extremely friendly service in a pleasant room with solid marble topped Britannia style tables and attractive china. This eating parlour has a comprehensive menu including grills such as gammon and egg, omelettes, or a traditional Yorkshire high tea – a savoury platter with bread and butter and a pot of tea. For something lighter there are scones, cinnamon toast, passion cake served hot with cream and, interestingly, carrot and honey cake was served with cheese and sliced apple; it worked well – the flavours being complimentary.

Open: 10am to 6pm every day except Christmas Day. Tel: 01535 642499

About the Area

Described by the late Arthur Mee (King's England, Yorkshire, West Riding) as an 'unlovely place; a 'grim place', with the surrounding countryside as a 'depressing scene', Haworth, or at least part of it, has obviously undergone a considerable metamorphosis in recent times. The village is, however, very much two places in one. Firstly, it is a basic industrial and pre-industrial settlement, founded on the bottom of the Worth Valley, where the stream provided power for the early textile mills, with houses and other properties progressively climbing the sides of the steep valley, reaching towards the bare windswept moorland on either side. It has to be said that this Haworth broadly confirms Mee's dismissive assessment.

But – high up the western hillside is Main Street, cobbled and almost traffic-free, restored to a broadly mid-19th century appearance, rising inexorably to the church and the adjacent parsonage which form the crown of visitor Haworth. The street is rich in inns, cafés and antique shops; visitors by the thousand come to pay homage to the Brontë's who lived at the Parsonage in this bleak moorside village. Without the presence of this sad but talented family, it is fair to surmise that the tourist industry would be non-existent. More will be said about the Brontë's in walk no.10, Haworth and Top Withins.

The best feature of valley bottom Haworth is the Keighley and Worth Valley Railway, a branch line which was opened in 1866, lost its passenger services in 1961 and was subsequently restored and

re-opened by dedicated volunteers as a major visitor attraction. The line climbs steeply from its junction with the Midland main line at Keighley to the terminus at Oxenhope. Most services are steam hauled and the smaller locomotives are working genuinely hard, not just putting on a show for the visitors, in climbing to Oxenhope. Services operate

Main Street, Haworth

on every weekend of the year and daily in summer, up to 12 workings daily, with special events such as the inevitable 'Santa Specials' and Enthusiasts' Weekends. Other features of the railway are the station shop at Haworth, open 364 days each year, locomotive depot at Haworth, superb Edwardian station at Oakworth, reserve collection of rolling stock at Oxenhope and a railway centre/carriage museum at Ingrow on the fringe of Keighley, open daily throughout the year.

The Walk

Walk by the roadside towards Haworth for 20 metres. Turn left along a wide grass track, passing an old notice concerning access to Brow Moor for 'air and exercise'. The track is fairly level, with abundant heather on either side. As the solitary wind turbine is approached, stay with the main track, bearing left and soon rising towards a belt of trees. Keighley is in view in the valley to the left. At the tree belt turn right at a 'T' junction along another well-used path, part of the 'Worth Way'. Descend to join a public road.

1. Turn left, then fork right in 50 metres into a farm trackway, turning right in 20 metres at a squeezer stile to go down a few steps to an access driveway. Turn left by a waymarked post to pass Duck Cottage and continue with a fence close on the right. At a small area of rough ground veer away from the fence and look carefully for a waymark on a post which shows the route through the rough ground, curving strongly to the right to a squeezer stile through the wall. Turn left by the side of the wall, cross a surfaced access drive, go through a small waymarked gate and pass behind a dwelling.

2. Go through two more gates and then a farm gate to reach another property and surfaced access drive. Turn left, uphill, to a stile signposted 'Worth Way Oxenhope' and turn right here.

    The track across a field is not well defined. Angle away from the wall on the left to make for the waymarked remains of a stile. Carry on to a gateway/squeezer stile. Turn right to follow a little green lane to a dwelling. Continue down the lane to a 'public footpath Worth Way' signpost, turning left over the waymarked stile. Start by the side of the hedge, then bear right to head for a stile in the far boundary wall. Keep the same line across the next field towards a gate/stile.

3. Leave the Worth Way here by turning right before the gate; stay beside the wall for about 70 metres then bear right, diagonally across the meadow, towards a stile in the bottom right corner, giving access to the public road. Turn right, along the roadside, cross over and turn left in 50 metres at a 'public bridleway' sign.

4. Go down a little flight of steps, staying close to the wall to descend over grass to a stile. Join a more major path and turn right to walk by the side of Bridgehouse Beck through pleasant woodland. Go over another stile and a wooden bridge to reach a lovely little packhorse bridge. Do not cross the bridge but bear right, uphill, following several waymarks, soon turning left across the front of a house and bearing further left to a little gate, followed by a narrow track close to a wall on the left. Descend some very old stone steps and pass a derelict cottage.

5. Go through an old iron kissing gate; from here much of the way is along the top of a built-up causeway, probably an old route to a mill. Cross a footbridge with integral kissing gate and continue. To the left is a former water channel, apparently a mill feed. There are more kissing gates before the path passes by the side of an old mill to join a public road in Haworth.

6. Turn left along Brow Road, then left again to cross the road bridge. To the right is the railway station, to the left are Bridgehouse Mills. Walk up the roadside pavement, quite steeply uphill. As this road bends to the right, fork left into cobbled Main Street, the pride of Haworth, and walk uphill towards the church. Right at the top, on the right, is Emma's Eating Parlour, recommended for refreshment.

After tea, turn right, up to the prominent tourist information centre. Fork right into Changegate. At the far end turn right into North Street, then left almost at once into Mytholmes Lane.

7. In 40 metres turn right into South View. Go through a gap in the wall at the bottom and turn right to take a good path downhill along the edge of open land, with a wall on the right.

At the bottom bear right, then left as the track forks, then left at a 'T' junction in a few metres to continue the descent. Reach a surfaced road and go left to the long footbridge over the railway, giving good views of the station area and some of the railway company's collection of rolling stock.

8. Bear right along the Station Road pavement, turning left into Brow Road at the end to start the steep ascent of the valley side. As Brow Road bends sharply to the right, turn left into Victoria Road. Take the second turning on the right, Dean Street, to walk up to the main road. Go straight across into a footpath, which soon becomes an old route between walls. Turn right at the top to join B6144.

9. Turn sharp left to walk towards the car park, passing the Three Sisters Hotel en route. The car park is a short distance beyond the top of the rise.

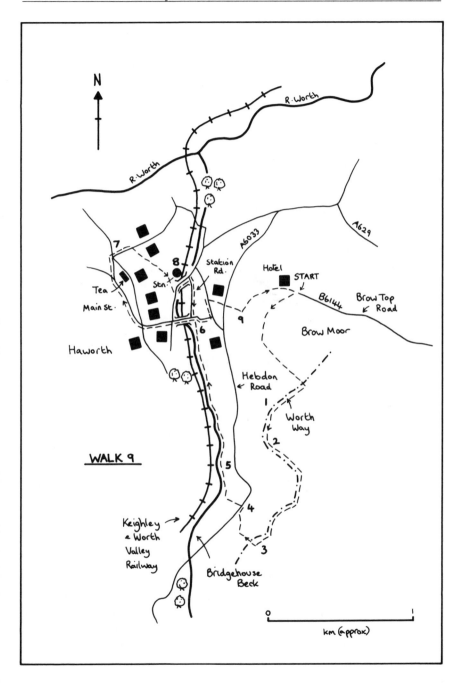

10. Haworth and the Brontë Country

Summary: A fine walk across the moorland immortalised by the Brontë sisters, visiting Top Withens, Brontë Falls, Brontë Bridge, Brontë Chair, The Parsonage and Haworth village. A fair amount of ascent and descent, but no really steep gradients and virtually all on moorland tracks and good footpaths. Top Withens is at 423m (1388 ft.). Use is made of parts of the Brontë Way and Pennine Way designated footpaths. A few stiles.

Length: 7¾ miles (12.4km)

Car Parking: One of many parking areas on the fringe of Penistone Hill, easily located beside public conveniences on Moorside Lane, a little more then half a mile south west of Haworth. Grid reference 019361.

Maps: Ordnance Survey Outdoor Leisure 21, South Pennines, 1:25,000 Ordnance Survey Landranger 104, Leeds and Bradford, 1:50,000.

The Tea Shop

From the many to choose from on this occasion we visited the Carousel Ice Cream Parlour. As expected, almost every variety of ice cream and ice cream dishes is served here. Try such temptations as the butterscotch and meringue surprise or the chocolate nut sundae – even diabetic ice cream is available. But it's not just ice cream – there are delicious cakes, sandwiches, bacon muffins, pancakes with fillings, toasted teacakes, and of course, tea, coffee, and cold drinks.

Open: 9.30am to 5pm every day all the year except Christmas Day and Boxing Day. Tel: 01535 644924

About the Area

General information about Haworth is included in walk no. 9, Haworth and the Worth Valley. The particular interest of the present walk rests firmly with the Brontë family, whose period of residence at the Parsonage has put Haworth very much on the tourist map.

Following a five-year period at Thornton, near Bradford, Patrick Brontë, his wife, and his six children took up residence in Haworth on his appointment as curate early in 1820. As Haworth church at that time was a chapel of ease, an outpost of the church at Bradford, the curate was in charge, occupying the spacious Parsonage. Patrick came from a poor Irish family, one of 10 children.

Misfortune was not long in coming to the Brontë family, two of the children, Maria and Elizabeth, soon dying of tuberculosis. The only son, Branwell, of whom much was expected by parents and by his surviving sisters, turned out to be a complete disappointment. Attempts to operate an art gallery in Bradford and to keep a mundane job on the railway both ended in failure. Excessive drinking, largely at the nearby Black Bull, and generally feckless behaviour, contributed to his subsequent notoriety and hastened his demise, again from tuberculosis, at the age of 31 years.

Even today it is very apparent that Haworth Church and Parsonage are situated close to the edge of the great expanse of moorland. This goes on for miles, over into Lancashire, a setting which conditioned the lives and the writing of the three remaining sisters – Emily, Anne and Charlotte; all eventually achieved literary fame within their own lifetimes. Their intimacy with this local landscape, its desolate gritstone buildings and the great sweep of the seemingly endless moor has left a legacy for exploration by today's visitor. For many, this is more evocative than the conventional visit to the Parsonage Museum, fascinating though that house and its contents may be. Even better for our present purpose is that some of the places which do most to conjure up the scenes in the novels are accessible only on foot.

The sad story of the lives of these talented young women is well known. Appointments as governesses and teachers at several places in Yorkshire were followed by a failed attempt to set up their own school in Haworth. During this period, the late 1830s and early 1840s, they were all writing in one form or another; a jointly written book of verse was published at their own expense. Just two copies were sold. However, after delays, the publication of novels was eventually successful – *Jane Eyre* (Charlotte), *Wuthering Heights* (Emily) and *Agnes Grey* (Anne) all appeared within a short space of time. *Jane Eyre* was particularly well reviewed and became a best seller, bringing widespread acclamation for Charlotte.

The enduring fame of the sisters rests on the success of a mere handful of novels; Emily and Anne had little time left to enjoy that success; Emily died first at 30 years of age, followed by Anne a few months later, during a visit to Scarborough. Charlotte soldiered on, still living with her father at Haworth. After a 10-year delay, brought about by her father's obstinate opposition, she married an assistant curate in 1854. The family tragedy continued; Charlotte soon conceived but the child was never born as she died in March 1855. Patrick, after burying a wife and six children, lived on alone until his death in 1861 at the age of 84 years.

The parish church of St. Michael and All Angels is not the church known to the Brontë's. Patrick Brontë's successor had the earlier church, apart from the bell tower, demolished in the 1870s and replaced by a larger church on the same site.

The walk set out below gives the opportunity to savour the Brontë experience in the most appropriate way.

The Walk

From the car park cross the public road and start down a broad, unsurfaced, track, over a cattle grid and on for about one mile, straight across the moor, soon passing Drop Farm, away to the left. Leeshaw Reservoir is down to the left. Harbour Lodge Farm comes into view, ahead. About 200 metres before the farm turn right at a signpost 'Brontë Falls and Top Withens'.

1. Go along a grass track and over a footbridge to another signpost. Turn left for 'Top Withens' and follow the path uphill to pass round the farm. At a signposted junction go straight on for 'Top Withens'. Harbour Hill is just above to the right as Top Withens comes into view on the far hillside. Continue along the top edge of the valley of an infant stream, cross the valley at a confluence, steeply down then up, and rise through bracken to join a major track.

2. Turn left for 'Top Withens'. If the route across the moor seems long and onerous, stride out and think of Emily Brontë.

The path, now with directions also in Japanese, is flagged as it climbs quite steeply to join the Pennine Way – the great grandfather of all British long-distance designated footpaths. Turn left to walk for 200 metres to reach Top Withens, where a plaque suggests that this incredibly remote farmhouse could have been the model for the home of the Earnshaws in 'Wuthering Heights'.

3. Start the return along the same track, turning right at the signpost for 'Haworth and the Brontë Falls'. At the next signpost, about half a mile from Top Withens, leave the outward route by forking left for 'Brontë Falls and Haworth'.

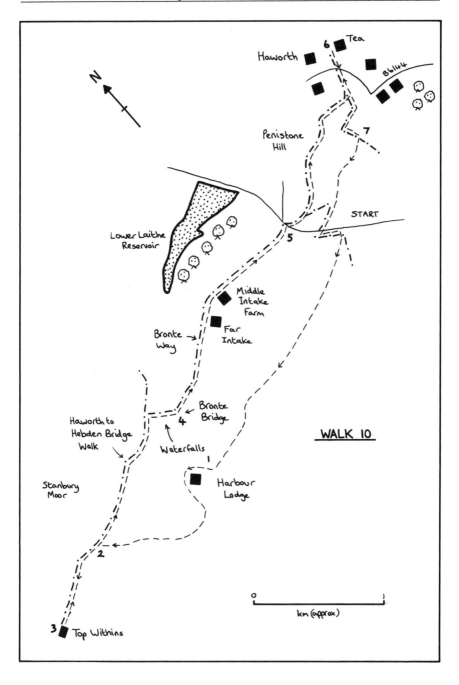

N

Tea

Haworth

6

B6144

Penistone
Hill

START

Lower Laithe
Reservoir

7

5

Middle
Intake
Farm

Far
Intake

Bronte
Way

Bronte
Bridge

WALK 10

Haworth to
Hebden Bridge
Walk

4

Waterfalls

Stanbury
Moor

Harbour
Lodge

2

0

km (approx)

3 Top Withins

The track is well-used and easy to follow, high along the side of the valley of the South Dean Beck.

Go over a waymarked ladder stile. Descend the valley side, turn right, through a kissing gate, and go down steeply to Brontë Bridge, destroyed in 1989 and rebuilt the following year. This is a charming spot, fine for picnics, with the 'Brontë Chair' adjacent.

4. Turn left at a signpost 'Brontë Way. Haworth 2½ miles'. In about 25 metres a glen-like little valley on the right has the Brontë Falls, not spectacular except after heavy rain.

Continue along a good track; the village in view left, ahead, is Stanbury. Apart from a short section over solid rock the track is first rate. Pass two ruined farmhouses, with Lower Laithe Reservoir occasionally in view below to the left, beyond a dense belt of trees. Reach a cattle grid, a gate and a signpost 'Haworth 1¼ miles' via Penistone Hill'.

5. Bear right to cross the grass to the public road. Turn right, up the road and, in 50 metres, turn left along an obvious stony track through the heather, heading for Penistone Hill. At a signposted junction turn left for 'Haworth 1' to pass a picnic area and car park. Follow a good track which keeps below the top of the hill, heading straight for Haworth, ignoring paths to right and left.

Go straight across a minor road and down a rough surfaced lane, signposted 'Haworth Church'. At the bottom turn left at a three-way sign to walk to the church, the Parsonage and the top end of Main Street. Turn right; the recommended tea shop is a little way down, on the left.

6. Return by the same route, passing the church, as far as the three-way signpost; turn left here along a narrow footpath signposted 'Oxenhope'. There are good views over Haworth, to the solitary wind turbine which is a dominant feature hereabouts. Go left then right to avoid Sowdens Farm before turning left along the bottom edge of a meadow. At a little gate in a wall, with waymark and signpost, turn right, up Dimples Lane towards 'Haworth Moor'.

7. At a minor road turn left for 40 metres then turn right, along a former quarry roadway. The roadway soon ends; continue along a narrow path, rising to join a better path; bear left. At a fork in 40 metres go left, along the side of a wall to reach a signposted junction; the top of Penistone Hill is close on the right. Keep left for 'Brontë Falls and Top Withens', through an extensive car parking area and down another quarry roadway. Keep left at a fork to make for the public conveniences and car park.

Short Walk – as a bonus, the following 3 mile (5km) walk, based on the Haworth end of the above route is suggested. In no way does this stroll substitute for the 'Brontë' walk, but it does give a flavour of the moor, a visit to Haworth and the opportunity to include another fine tea shop.

From a pay and display car park in Haworth village (that at the very top, three minutes walk from the tourist information centre, grid reference 029374, is

The Brontë Bridge, near Haworth

suggested), follow the return route past the church and Sowden Farm set out in the main walk. Pass the public conveniences, cross over the minor road, Moorside Lane, and head for the signposted Drop Farm, a splendidly situated place for refreshments.

Return to Moorside Lane, turn left for a few metres and then turn right to head up the former quarry roadway. Keep left of the large car parking areas, rising to the point where our original path comes in on the left at a signpost. From this point follow the directions given in the main walk to return to Haworth.

Another Tea Shop

Discovered after the main walk had been completed, the authors could not resist finding space to include Drop Farm Tea Rooms in this book. However, the opening hours are restricted and it is therefore all the more surprising to see such a large and comprehensive menu. One may order anything from a roast dinner to a teacake! In between are offerings such as the ploughman's platter comprising a variety of cheese, pork pie, plus roll and butter. Alternatively, the pork pie can be served with mushy peas and mint sauce! Homemade cakes and scones are always available and a set afternoon tea is also listed.

Open: 12pm to 5pm on Wednesday and Thursdays (closes at 4.30pm in winter) and from 12pm to 5.30pm on Sundays. Open throughout the year. If in any doubt, we suggest a telephone call before starting out. Tel: 01535 645297

11. Stanbury and Ponden Mill

Summary: An unpretentious but enjoyable walk based on Ponden Mill, through agricultural countryside, visiting the straggling stone village of Stanbury. Several stiles, some cattle-churned ground and steep but not very long ascents. Some rights of way are rather overgrown in places. Almost a mile of generally quiet roadside walking.

Length: 3 miles (4.8km)

Car Parking: Always assuming that walkers intend to use the refreshment facilities at the mill, Ponden is the only realistic choice. Of course, the bargains evident en route to the café may well prove to be irresistible, at least to lady walkers! Grid reference 999373.

Maps: Ordnance Survey Outdoor Leisure 21, South Pennines, 1:25,000 Ordnance Survey Landranger 104, Leeds and Bradford, (part) Landranger 103, Blackburn and Burnley (part), 1:50,000.

The Tea Shop

It is necessary to find a reserve of energy to reach 'The Weavers'Buttery' at Ponden Mill for it is through the retail area and upstairs. Understandably you are requested to leave rucksacks and boots in the entrance porch. The café is most welcoming with good decor and attractive lighting. Just about everything is served here, from a cup of coffee to three course meals, with pleasant waitress service. For tea there are delicious cakes – try the Bakewell cake – it is scrumptious! The traditional afternoon tea includes sandwiches. Should you visit at lunch time, there is a choice of about six main dishes such as lasagne or beef steak pie – all dishes are freshly prepared on the premises. Cold platter, sandwiches, and cakes available at all times.

Open: 10am to 5pm every day and 11am to 4.30pm on Sundays. Tel: 01535 643500.

About the Area

The road from Haworth to Colne, passing through the village of Stanbury, provides one of the minor, comparatively little used,

Pennine crossings. It passes over the moorland at a maximum height of 347m (1139ft). Until a little way beyond Ponden Reservoir, the countryside is marginal agriculture, laced with stone walls, set between great moors to north and south.

Late 18th/early 19th century industry pushed its way up this valley of the infant River Worth, as evidenced by Ponden Mill and the substantial ruin a little way downstream which is a feature of this walk. Another feature of the walk is the great age of some of the farm buildings. Ponden Mill has a new lease of life, smartly renovated as the flagship store for the Ponden Mill trading enterprise. Stanbury itself is pleasant but unremarkable, whilst Ponden Hall, beyond the mill, is believed to be the 'Thrushcross Grange' of Emily Brontë's 'Wuthering Heights'.

The Walk

From Ponden Mill car park, walk past the mill and the further car park at the rear and continue along a surfaced lane with a 'Ponden Hall ½ mile' signpost. The stream on the right is the outfall from Ponden Reservoir, the headwaters of the River Worth. Follow the roadway as it bends to the left to rise to the top of the dam. Join the Pennine Way at a four-way signpost. In 25 metres leave the Pennine Way by turning right to cross the dam at a 'Scar Top ¼ mile' signpost. The reservoir is a fine sheet of water with the partly wooded Ponden Clough cutting deeply into the high moorland.

1. Reach Colne Road and turn left, passing Scar Top Farm and cottages. Turn right in about 100 metres to ascend a concrete driveway to Dean Field Farm, protected by a dense tree belt which includes some decorative conifers. Just before reaching the farm, go through a gate with a blue arrow, facing you on the right, then go to the right, along the far side of a fence, over some rough ground for about 60 metres, heading for a small gate.

2. Go through and then bear to the right across a narrow meadow to another gate/squeezer stile. Continue over roughish ground towards farm buildings. Go to the left to pass behind this farm, then turn right, to a gate. Go through and turn left along a rough surfaced access driveway. Turn right at a junction in 200 metres to descend past Pitcher Clough Farm and join a minor public road, Oldfield Lane.

Turn left to amble along this road for a longish half mile, with views across the valley to Stanbury and Haworth Moor, very much Brontë country. The road ascends past rows of cottages and a scrap yard to reach the hamlet of Oldfield, with a school dated 1877.

3. Forty metres after the school, turn right between stone gate posts to start the descent of the valley side on a surfaced access drive, forking right on to a gravelled road in 100 metres. Pass close to a farm on the right, continue down a green lane and over a stile, then down an overgrown grass lane to a decrepit ladder stile.

    Those who fear for limb, if not life, might prefer to climb over the adjacent fence. Head for the valley bottom along the right-hand edge of a meadow, with a burbling little stream on the right. Towards the bottom end of a broken wall bear left, then go down to a gate and through an open gate to reach the bank of the River Worth.

    Turn right and go over a stile in 50 metres. Note the spiked railings, surely an 'urban' feature, related to the former mill. Bear right to walk beside the wall of the mill ruin, then left at the far end to go up a grassy ramp by a diminishing wall. The former mill pond is now a reedy swamp. Bear right, along the top of an old retaining wall, turning left in a few metres to find a reasonably dry route through the reeds and to rise towards a fence, ahead.

    The steep slope is cattle churned and messy; head for an open gateway, well to the left. Go through and continue the ascent alongside an ancient sunken lane between broken walls. As the lane disappears, carry on towards farm buildings. Fifty metres or so before the buildings bear left to a gate. Go through and round the end of a building, turning left again to reach the main road in Stanbury, near to the school. The bulk of the village, including two inns, is to the left.

4. Turn right to walk by the side of the road for nearly 300 metres. Ignore a signposted route to Top Withens, but bear left as the road dips to the right, to follow a good looking path, with fine views to the reservoir and to the Old Silent Inn and Ponden Mill, below. Go down to the right, to a farm; pass along the front of the building, through three gates in total, and continue along the bottom of a meadow, with a wall on the right.

5. In 80 metres turn right, just before a very old agricultural building, and descend towards the mill. Turn right at the far end of a wall, then left in a few metres to go down a meadow, with a broken stone wall on the left, to a squeezer stile in the bottom corner. Bear slightly right to a wooden stile in 30 metres and go down to the road, reached close to a bridge. Go through another squeezer stile and turn left to cross the bridge and then left again into the Ponden Mill driveway.

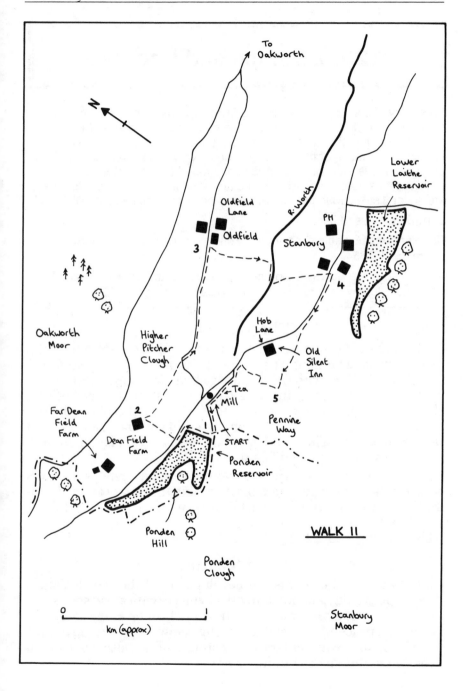

To Oakworth

N

Lower Laithe Reservoir

Oldfield Lane

Oldfield

3

R. Worth

PH

Stanbury

4

Oakworth Moor

Higher Pitcher Clough

Hob Lane

Old Silent Inn

Tea Mill

5

Far Dean Field Farm

2

Dean Field Farm

1

START

Pennine Way

Ponden Reservoir

Ponden Hill

WALK 11

Ponden Clough

0   1

km (approx)

Stanbury Moor

12. Oxenhope and Nab Hill

Summary: An attractive walk linking Oxenhope with the nearby moorland to the south, including Nab Hill at a little more than 450 metres (nearly 1,500ft.). Despite this considerable height, there are no really steep gradients and much of the ascent is along a very minor road, chosen in preference to lengths of rough and vague moorland path. Roadside walking totals about two miles. There are no problems underfoot but there are several stiles. Much of the return is along part of the 'Brontë Way'.

Length: 6 miles (9.5km)

Car Parking: Sizeable car park at Oxenhope railway station. Grid reference 033354.

Maps: Ordnance Survey Outdoor Leisure 21, South Pennines, 1:25,000 Ordnance Survey Landranger 104, Leeds and Bradford, 1:50,000.

The Tea Shop

Quite a different venue for tea! A converted railway coach, with original seating and authentic photographs, situated by the platform at Oxenhope Station, with the advantage that you can watch the railway activity whilst enjoying well-earned refreshments. The buffet is clean, smart, and the service is friendly. Good choice of hot drinks, and cold drinks are obtainable from the chiller cabinet. Hot and cold savoury pies, sandwiches, crisps, and a selection of cakes, including really moist old-fashioned jam roll.

Open: This facility is provided by volunteers and operates in accordance with the railway time-table. Days and times vary according to the time of year. Definitely open for steam weekends, bank holidays, school holidays. Advisable to telephone or consult up-to-date time-table. Tel: 01535 645214

About the Area

Close to the head of industrial development of the Worth Valley, Oxenhope is a tidy, quietly attractive, village, with a few shops and inns. There are surviving mill buildings but the prevailing ambience is now of a peaceful settlement nestling below a great sweep of high moorland. Reservoirs and the connecting conduits also make a contribution to this sparse but fine landscape.

Oxenhope – Keighley & Worth Valley Railway

The attractive terminus of the preserved Keighley and Worth Valley Railway is at Oxenhope, with a museum which houses a reserve collection of rolling stock. More information about the railway can be found in walk no. 9, Haworth and the Worth Valley.

The Walk

From the railway station walk up Station Road and turn left into Harry Lane. Go across the main road into Dark Lane, uphill. Turn right at the first junction to follow a back road downhill. Go straight across the main road to rise along a minor road, with a factory and its chimney on the left.

1. As the road bends to the right, go straight on into Hill House Lane. As this road ends, continue along a rising lane between walls, which soon becomes a narrower footpath. Reach a broad, stony, roadway by a house and turn left. Continue along this broad track past more dwellings, bending to the right to rise along the side of a small valley.
    The track soon bends quite sharply to the right; go round this bend for a few metres, then strike off diagonally to the left, up to an obvious gap in a wall.

2. Go through, pass waymarks, cross over an old water conduit, then turn left through a little gate. The lightly worn path over grass is still ascending

quite steeply. Keep close to the wall on the left, go over a stile, then through a waymarked gate to reach a very minor public road, Nab Water Lane. Turn left.

3. The surroundings are now open moorland, with fine and extensive views. Follow the lane for about one mile, mostly uphill. There are moorland paths, but the road provides the preferred walking route. Pass a conduit and associated works. Warley Moor Reservoir is visible to the right. After a left bend, rise towards the road summit and turn left at the second 'public footpath' signpost, just below old mineral working spoil heaps.

4. Go over the stile to follow a clear path over rough grass, climbing diagonally to the edge of Nab Hill, much scarred by the spoil of long forgotten mineral workings. The path winds sinuously and invitingly among the hummocks; half a mile or so to the right some of a modern wind farm is apparent and, as a cairn and a shelter are approached, the views down the Worth Valley extend as far as Keighley.

5. The narrow path continues along the edge and past more former industrial remains as Thornton Moor Reservoir comes into view. Keep left at a fork, now descending towards the reservoir, then bear left to a farm gate giving access to a major track, Hambleton Lane, apparently an old drove road. Turn left, downhill.

6. Go through a gate to head for a signpost, less than 100 metres beyond. At the signpost go straight on 'public path Brontë Way', downhill over grass. Pass a waymark on an old gatepost, follow an old wall on the right to another waymark, on a stone post, aiming straight for Leeming Reservoir. Turn left at this post towards yet another waymark on a post, in 50 metres. Turn right—there is a broken wall close on the right. Cross over a conduit and a ladder stile and continue the descent past another waymark; the track is now obvious on the ground.
   Descend to cross a culvert and continue along a well defined path. Cross a plank bridge and stay beside a wall, with the reservoir to the right. Go through two squeezer stiles, then a conventional stile over a wall, to continue down to a gate, a signpost, another squeezer stile and a tarmac surfaced farm road.

7. Carry on towards Oxenhope, to a gate/squeezer stile and go through a farm gate, now level with the reservoir dam, to take a track signposted 'Oxenhope ½ mile'. Rise to the main Denholme Road and turn left along the roadside pavement.
   On reaching the crossroads passed on the outer route, continue along Station Road through the village. Cross a major road and go straight ahead, passing a Queen Victoria post box on the way to the station buffet and the car park.

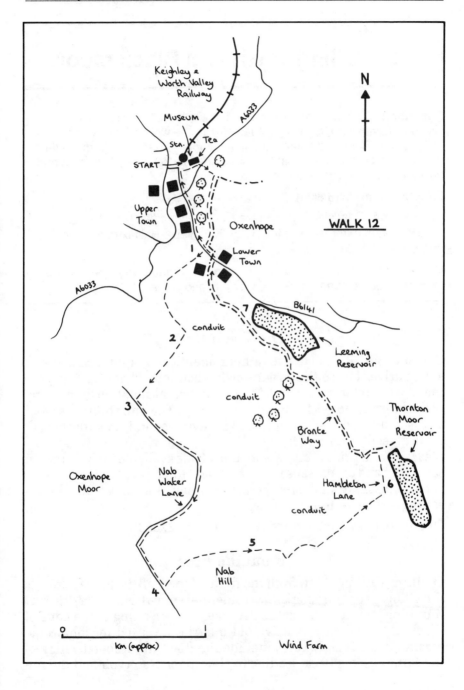

Keighley &
Worth Valley
Railway

Museum

Stn.   Tea

START

Upper
Town

Oxenhope

WALK 12

1

Lower
Town

A6033

A6033

B6141

conduit

2

7

Leeming
Reservoir

3

conduit

Bronte
Way

Thornton
Moor
Reservoir

Oxenhope
Moor

Nab
Water
Lane

Hambleton
Lane

6

conduit

5

4

Nab
Hill

0   1

km (approx)   Wind Farm

---

13. Cullingworth and Black Moor

Summary: A fine walk around the Cullingworth area, without actually visiting Cullingworth, combining Black Moor, the wooded valley of the Milking Hole Beck and some agricultural countryside. Apart from a little mud, no problems with the lanes and footpaths. Relatively few stiles and only a short length of roadside footpath.

Length: 4¼ miles (6.8km)

Car Parking: Roadside layby on the B6429, immediately to the north of the junction of that road with the A629, Keighley – Halifax road. Grid reference, 064355.

Maps: Ordnance Survey Outdoor Leisure 21, South Pennines, 1:25,000. Ordnance Survey Landranger 104, Leeds and Bradford, 1:50,000.

The Tea Shop

Coldspring Mill is small and rather romantic. It is approached down a long drive. The setting is extremely pleasant and one can imagine that it was preferable to work in a mill in a rural situation than in one of the larger factories in an industrial town. The mill shop sells wool at discounted prices, patterns, skirt lengths, and haberdashery – quite a needlewoman's haven! The tea rooms are attractive, service pleasant, and prices very reasonable. Meals available include prawn salad, egg and chips, sausages, bacon and tomato sandwiches; cakes can be chosen from the refrigerated display. A good café in a lovely setting – some outdoor seating.

Open: 10am to 4pm every day. Tel: 01535 275646

About the Area

Omitting Cullingworth from the route of the walk is no great loss as the village is an unremarkable residential sprawl. However, the surrounding countryside is attractive, agriculture rising to the edge of Black Moor, where extensive old quarries are used for motorbike scrambling. Other features include the fine little wooded valley of the Milking Hole Beck, leading to Hewenden Reservoir and the impressive curving viaduct, 120 feet high, with 17 arches spaced at 50 foot intervals, which carries a now defunct railway line.

Coldspring Mill is a compact former mill building on the Manywells Beck, from which power was obtained; the present chimney is obvious evidence of a later conversion to steam.

The Walk

Cross the road to a signpost 'public bridleway' and set off along an excellent level track with trees on the left and an old wall on the right, soon passing a refuse tip in former quarries on the left. Cullingworth village is partially visible in the valley bottom, left/ahead. Descend gently, crossing a bridge over a disused railway line before reaching the public road, the B6144.

1. Turn right, along the roadside pavement, passing a long terrace of cottages, Springfield Terrace; Hewenden is the hamlet visible on the hill, ahead. Two hundred metres after joining the road, turn right at a lane with a 'public footpath' sign and a broken tarmac surface.

2. Cross the old railway line at a dismantled bridge and head for East Manywells Farm, with good views of the viaduct. Rise through the farm, bearing a little right, uphill, to a gate. The farm area may well be muddy. The route continues as a walled lane, the views improving progressively. About 200 metres after the farm leave the broad track as it bends to the right, uphill, by forking left to stay close to a wall.

   Go to a waymarked squeezer stile beside a gate and continue, slightly downhill, soon along a green lane between walls, then through a gate to rise gently along the bottom edge of a meadow to an easy stile. Descend a path over rough grass, soon forking right.

3. The path along Milking Hole Beck valley side is narrow but adequate. Cross a broken wall to reach woodland, gorse, hawthorn and bramble initially, then silver birch. The path threads its way through to a waymarked squeezer stile at a wall. Rise gently to approach a two arch bridge carrying a main pipeline across a narrow valley. Bear left here to rise towards the main A629 road and dwellings. Go over a wooden stile by an overgrown gate and through a little gate to reach the road.

4. Cross over to a 'public footpath' signpost almost opposite and continue along the drive to Field Head House. Pass the side of the house and go through Field Head Farm to a green lane between walls. Go through an old kissing gate and along the bottom edge of a field then through another kissing gate to reach a stony lane by Copperas House. Turn right to pass some very old properties, now going slightly uphill to a minor public road.

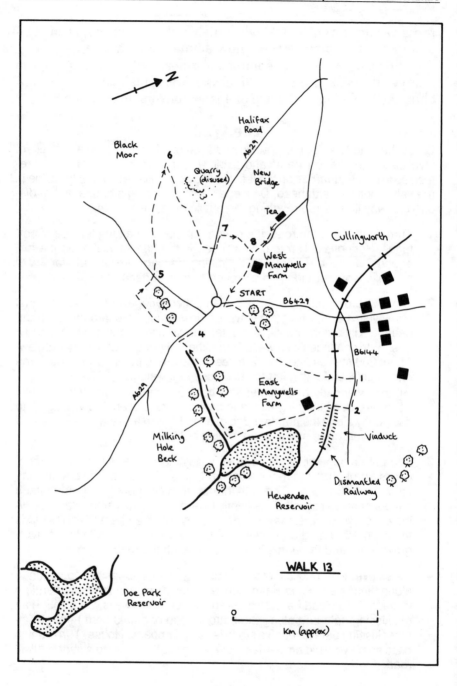

WALK 13

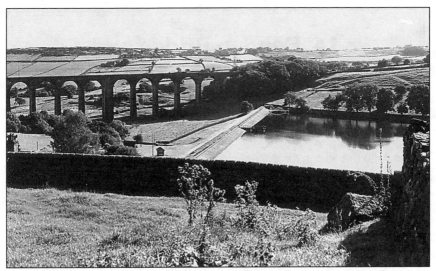

Landscape near Cullingworth

5. Go across to a 'public footpath' sign and waymarked stile to start the walk across Black Moor. At first the path is not entirely clear, but keep to the grass between banks of heather, aiming a little to the left of the solitary wind turbine. The track soon becomes better defined. On reaching a major fork keep to the right. (the left fork heads for a visible caravan site). At a junction marked by a large upright stone, turn sharp right.

6. Pass above major quarry workings and descend to the main road, reached through a modern gate. Coldspring Mill is now visible in the valley bottom ahead. Cross the road, turning left for 50 metres to a 'public footpath' sign. Go over the wall on a stepped stile.

7. The ground ahead is much disturbed by quarry workings and dumping; the right of way keeps a fairly straight line, as indicated by the signpost. However, aim a little to the right of Cold Spring Mill to descend to a waymark on a post, near the bottom fringe of the spoil. Continue to another post by a gateway in the wall on the right and proceed to a partially ruinous agricultural building. Keep to the left of the building, go through a gate and follow the rather overgrown access track. In 70 metres go over a stile and a railway sleeper bridge over a ditch to join an old walled lane.

8. Turn left to descend to Coldspring Mill. Return up the same lane, pass point *8.* and continue the gentle ascent past West Manywells Farm to join a stony roadway and rise to the B6249 road. Turn left to reach the layby in 100 metres.

14. Hebden Bridge and Hardcastle Crags Estate

Summary: The basic walk set out in full below connects the middle of Hebden Bridge and the National Trust Hardcastle Estate car parking areas, with public conveniences, picnic area and information boards. To reach the crags themselves, via Gibson Mill, a further distance, out and back, of almost three miles is required. Having said that, this walk up and down the lower part of the Hebden Water is attractive, a gentle stroll in a steep sided wooded valley on good tracks. A rich array of industrial remains is apparent, particularly relating to the water powered mills which filled this part of the valley from the late 1700s. There is a flight of steps which some walkers might find to be rather awkward, but no other impediment. Two variations of route are suggested; these add somewhat to the effort required. Part of the route is along the designated Haworth to Hebden Bridge Walk. It is relevant to consider the use of the reasonable bus service which connects Hebden Bridge with the National Trust car parking area, either to reduce the basic return walk to a 1½ mile stroll or to incorporate the extension to the mill and the crags without having to walk almost 6 miles in total.

Length: 3 miles (4.8km) – the basic walk.

Car Parking: Hebden Bridge centre. Garden Street free car park, as walk no. 16, is recommended. Grid reference 994273.

Maps: Ordnance Survey Outdoor Leisure 21, South Pennines, 1:25,000. Ordnance Survey Landranger 103, Blackburn and Burnley, 1:50,000.

The Tea Shop

Following the walk, we called in at the Innovation Café in Bridge Mill. Built around the middle of the eighteenth century, the creeper-covered mill is an attractive feature in the centre of Hebden Bridge. From the windows of the café there are views of the river and weir and it is hoped that the water wheel will be rebuilt at some time in the future. The menu is very comprehensive; one speciality is pancakes – sweet or savoury, vegetarian, chilli, lemon and syrup; the permutations are vast! Hot dishes, sandwiches, cakes, biscuits, and scones are all available. Drinks include tea and coffee – filtered

Hebden Bridge: converted former mill

or cafetiere – by the mug or cup, and cold drinks such as Orangina or ginger beer.

Open: 10am to 5pm Monday to Saturday and 1pm to 5pm on Sunday all the year. Tel: 01422 844160.

About the Area

Hebden Bridge is briefly described in walk no. 16, Hebden Bridge and Stoodley Pike. The Hardcastle Crags Estate, protected and cared for by the National Trust, is a lovely area of steep sided valleys, woodland, rocky ravines and rushing water. Crimsworth Dean, which is the valley to the north of the car parks, was planted and landscaped in the 19th century by Lord Savile to provide an attractive approach to his shooting estate on the adjacent moorland. Close to the heart of Hebden Dale and the crags is the 19th century Gibson Mill. The best access to the Mill and its surrounding area is along part of the Haworth to Hebden Bridge Walk, about one mile through the woods from the car parks which are the destination of the walk set out below. A return can be made by another path which stays close to the side of Hebden Water for most of the distance.

The estate is noted for wildlife, including the claimed presence of the increasingly rare red squirrel.

The Walk

From the Tourist Information Centre turn left to walk along Bridge Gate. In about 100 metres turn left over an old packhorse bridge, the original 'Hebden Bridge', to cross Hebden Water, the first of several crossings on this walk. Pass the front of the Hole in the Wall Inn, then turn right, to pass the Health Centre.

1. Bear right, then left, along Valley Road, passing a car park which is used as a market area each Wednesday, and public conveniences. Cross Hebden Water again; set well back to the right is Nutcliffe Mill, a significant place in the industrial development of the town. Turn left at a children's playground, then right and left again to walk past modern terraced cottages and reach Foster Bridge, a lovely little packhorse bridge.

2. Cross, then turn right immediately at a 'Riverside path. Hardcastle Crags' signpost. The scenery quite suddenly becomes very rural, with Hebden Water bustling along on the right, and a good level path to the Bowling Club. Cross Hebden Water (the fourth time) on a footbridge and turn left along the top of a causeway, with the stream on the left and a dry mill leat on the right. Pass a stepped weir to reach an unsurfaced road.

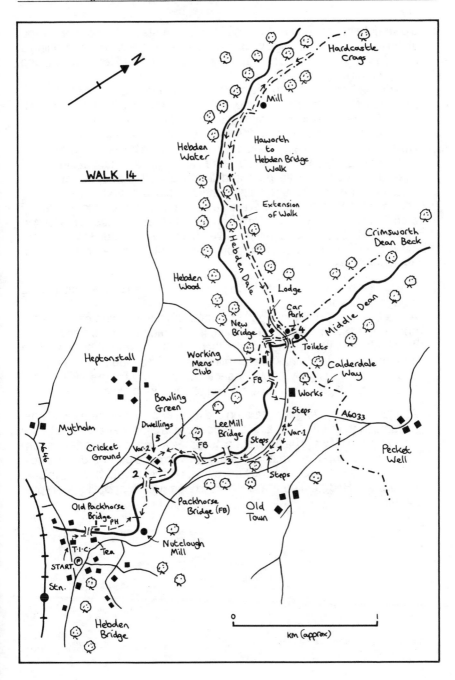

3. Go straight across and up the flight of irregular steps. Turn left at the top along a broad track through woodland, just below the valley road, rising a little. Join the public road by Raw Holme Farm and turn left to walk along the road for about 500 metres.

A variation here has been provided by the National Trust – a path through the lower fringe of Spring Wood, rising up steps and then winding between the trees before descending a few steps back to the road. The path is rough in places, but about 300 metres of road walking is avoided.

Go along the road to a left fork, down a lane with a broken surface, soon turning left to pass a house. In 50 metres turn right at a 'Hardcastle Crags' sign, go through a little gate and follow a well worn path across a meadow. Turn left through a little gate and cross a footbridge over the stream. Continue along the riverside path, passing Midgehole Working Men's Club before reaching New Bridge and a stony vehicular track up to join the public road close to the conveniences and the bus stop. The car parks are to the left, the information boards, maps etc. being situated in the higher parking areas.

4. The same route can be used for the return to Hebden Bridge, but there is a suggested variation:

At the bowling green turn right, pass through the adjacent parking area and continue along the access drive. In 120 metres look carefully for a small retaining wall on the left and then rake back very sharply along a narrow path, rising behind the bowling green. The path remains narrow and has some slightly sporting sections as it climbs the valley side. Reach a small group of houses and a chapel-like building.

5. At a junction go straight ahead, on the level to pass between dwellings, keeping slightly left at the far end. Proceed with a low wall on the left, now enjoying fine views. The track soon becomes a walled lane; after a sharp left turn at a junction, descend steeply over cobbles and down a few steps to Foster Bridge. Retrace the outward route to return to the middle of Hebden Bridge. The tea shop at Bridge Mill is opposite George's Square.

15. Heptonstall

Summary: Centred on Heptonstall village, this walk is a little more demanding than the mileage would indicate. However, the fine routes along the top edge of Colden Clough, part of the Calderdale Way, and that above Hebden Dale, more than compensate for the effort involved and these are by no means the only sections with wonderful views. The paths are very mixed; there are significant sections which are rough, with some rocks and tree roots underfoot requiring concentration. Otherwise, field paths, farm driveways and a little quiet public road. Many stiles but no prolonged or difficult ascents.

Length: 4¾ miles (7.6km)

Car Parking: Heptonstall is a traffic restricted village, with just two car parks. Recommended is a large free car park at the social club, at the southern tip of the village. Grid reference 987277. Note the special traffic arrangement giving access to Heptonstall from Hebden Bridge.

Maps: Ordnance Survey Outdoor Leisure 21, South Pennines, 1:25,000. Ordnance Survey Landranger 103, Blackburn and Burnley, 1:50,000.

The Tea Shop

Unique and special are the adjectives that come to mind for the award winning shop known as 'May's'. We particularly wished to include a walk including Heptonstall and were delighted to find that refreshments are available here. The shop is way out in a most unlikely situation. However, being close to the route of the Pennine Way it is an oasis for long distance walkers and is open from dawn to dusk with the exception of Christmas Day. It must be admitted that this is not a tea shop – no indoor seating – just benches outside; in poor weather walkers are welcome to take shelter in an out-building but it would obviously be preferable to visit on a fine day. Nothing is too much trouble here and one can have tea, coffee, cold drinks, cakes, hot pies, sandwiches, or ice creams. The shop is fascinating – tiny but selling everything from newspapers to a rocking horse!

Open: Almost all the time! – say 9am to 9pm every day except Christmas Day – just ring the bell. Tel: 01422 842897

About the Area

An early industrial village on a hilltop overlooking Hebden Bridge, Heptonstall is a remarkable survival. The largely weaving industry was of the 'cottage' variety, pre-dating the industrial revolution. With the advent of the use of water power and subsequently steam power and the gathering of the industry into mills of ever increasing size the village, far away from suitable watercourses, soon became a backwater. And so it has remained; fortunately unscathed by unsuitable modern development and now enjoying protected status as a Conservation Area, Heptonstall is a considerable visitor attraction. The hilltop is actually the narrow end of a ridge separating the deep valleys of Colden Clough and Hebden Water.

Within the village are two inns and the odd shop, the former Cloth Hall in Towngate, the former Dungeon in the village centre car park and a fine Methodist Chapel, off Northgate. The latter, built in 1764, is one of the oldest Methodist chapels in the world still in use.

Weavers' Square, once the site of houses, is surfaced to display different types of paving common in Yorkshire.

Adjacent to the Square are the remains of an 800-year-old church, most of what is now visible being of the 15th century, abandoned after damage to the tower during a storm in 1847. Its replacement stands close by, a large impressive building of 1854, in a broadly

Heptonstall, West Laithe

15th century style. Near the porch of the old church is the grave of David Hartley, the 'king of the coiners' heavily involved in a great counterfeiting conspiracy, which resulted in him being hanged at York in 1770.

Standing next to the old church is the former Grammar School, founded in 1642, now used as a museum, with much of the original school equipment on show. Opening times are limited, normally afternoons on Saturdays, Sundays and Bank Holidays from Easter to the end of October.

The surrounding countryside is upland farming, with relatively small farms, closely spaced.

The Walk

Walk along the unsurfaced lane opposite the car park entrance, behind houses, to reach a surfaced road. Turn sharp left to follow 'public footpath. Colden'; there is also a Calderdale Way waymark.

1. Go straight through a modern housing estate, built sympathetically in reconstructed stone, soon reaching the edge of the scarp overlooking Colden Clough, a very impressive viewpoint. Turn right to head for outcropping rocks. The path is narrow but delightful for some distance, but do take care with young children! The views are over the Clough, Mytholm village below, and the western part of Hebden Bridge. Stoodley Pike is also in view. The path enters light woodland, birch then oak and beech, enlivened in late summer by banks of heather. Join a surfaced road.

2. Turn left, downhill, forking right in 150 metres along a waymarked path, initially level. Rise over old stone paving, between walls, to a junction with a seat. Continue over a waymarked stile and along a paved causeway, heading for a farm.
Go over a stile and pass the house. Continue along a stony drive to a farm entrance gate less than 200 metres further and turn right, over a stile, then along a rather overgrown length of path, mercifully short.

3. Go over another stile and along the edge of a meadow, with a wall on the left, heading for a large farmstead. Go over a narrow stile and join the farm access road. Turn right, then left in 40 metres along the access drive to the next farm. As the track bends to the left, down into the farm yard, turn right at a 'footpath' sign to go up a step, passing a waymark on an electricity pole, then over two further stiles within a few metres. Across the fields to the right are some rather isolated terraces of cottages. Note a waymark on a post immediately after a stile and go straight on. Pass the front of yet another farmhouse, go through a broken wall and then a gate

on the right to enter a small field. Keep left, along the bottom of the field and go round the end of a gate on the left to reach Sutcliffe House.

4. Turn right, up the access drive, then left in 50 metres through a gap in a stone wall, up three steps and along a minor, overgrown, path which passes behind some post World War II system-built council houses. Go down a few steps to a farm access driveway, part of the Pennine Way, then up a few steps to continue through two little gates and join the public road.

5. Turn left then, in 70 metres, turn right at a not very distinct squeezer stile and little gate to follow an old causeway path, through three more little gates and a squeezer stile, to reach the large farmstead of Colden. Turn right to walk through the farm, then rise quite steeply. As the track bends to the left, look out for a footpath raking back to the right, 35 metres after the bend. Follow this path to reach the refreshments which are available at the remarkable multi-purpose shop at High Gate.

    From High Gate continue to a very minor road; walk on for about 200 metres to the junction with the Pennine Way. Turn left to go uphill to a gate beside Long High Top. In a further 40 metres fork right along a little path leading to a gate, then a lane between damaged walls, followed by the Long High Top access drive. This drive provides a fine easy walking route descending along the top of the high ground separating the two valleys, the extensive views including Heptonstall and its church. Eighty metres before reaching a minor road, go left – there is a post minus its sign.

6. Initially our route is now a grass cart track. Reach a seat on the left and turn right. Do not go through the obvious field gate, but follow a narrow path on the right which keeps close to a wall on the left, descending gently, with banks of heather on the right. Pass another post which seems to have had its sign removed and proceed to the minor road at Popples hamlet.

7. Turn left for 20 metres then turn right down a cobbled way. In 20 metres go through a little gate on the right and down the edge of a field, with a wall on the left. Go over a stile at the end of the wall, then through a little gate at the edge of Hebden Wood. Turn right to walk for more than half a mile high on the valley side of Hebden Dale, with fearsomely steep slopes on the left in places, including a few crags. Parts of the path are awkward, with some overgrowth , mud and a few tree roots. More major paths join from the left; avoid any descending track and do not be tempted by either of the tracks which head away from the wood, to the right. At the end of this apparently very long half a mile, go up a few steps

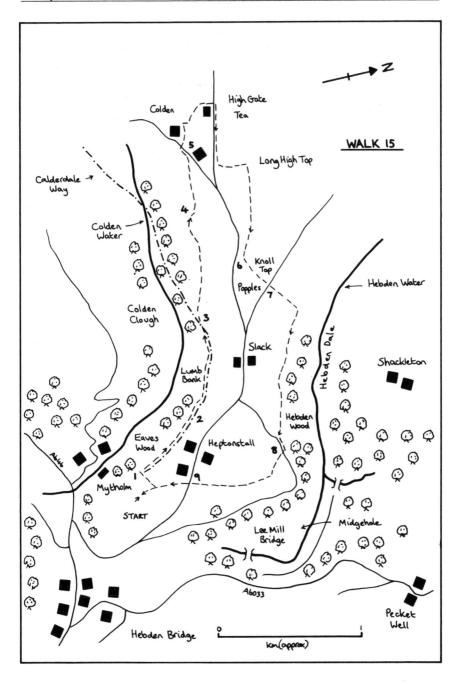

WALK 15

at the end of a wall and along the bottom edge of a large meadow. Go over a stile to a very minor road.

8. Turn left and, in 45 metres, turn right at a 'public footpath' sign to go up steps and through a squeezer stile. Bear slightly left across a meadow to an obvious easy squeezer stile and carry on across the next meadow to a gateway. Bear right, with the wall on the right, up to a gate/stile and follow the walled green lane which leads directly into the centre of Heptonstall.

9. Pass some surprisingly surviving post World War II pre-fabs, hopefully with time to spare for a look at least some of Heptonstall's fine features, all close at hand.
For the car park turn left, downhill, at Towngate, pass the White Lion Inn, and turn right into Church Yard Bottom, passing the museum in the Old Grammar School building. Bear left to go straight across a residential road and rejoin the outward route, forking left to pass behind houses, directly to the car park

16. Hebden Bridge and Stoodley Pike

Summary: Even without the challenging focal point of Stoodley Pike, this would still be a very good walk. A half mile pull up the minor road to Horsehold is followed by a more gentle upland walk to the Pike and a return route which keeps most of the hard earned altitude for a considerable distance. There are a few rough sections of footpath, otherwise very good tracks and green lanes generally. Several stiles.

Length: 6¼ miles (10km)

Car Parking: Several public car parks in the middle of Hebden Bridge. The free car park at Garden Street is convenient. Grid reference 994273.

Maps: Ordnance Survey Outdoor Leisure 21, South Pennines, 1:25,000. Ordnance Survey Landranger 103, Blackburn and Burnley, 1:50,000.

The Tea Shop

Walkers are assured of a very warm welcome at Coffee Cali. This café, recently opened by Jan Garvey, deserves to be successful. Although appearing to be quite small, there is extra seating upstairs and a limited amount in the small courtyard. The decor is stylishly simple with modern Italian designed furniture and wooden floors. The menu includes excellent coffee of many varieties, tea, fruit teas, hot chocolate, and other drinks; to eat there is a variety of cakes, Danish pastries, muffins, grilled ciabatta sandwiches, and hot dishes as listed on the board. For those wishing to linger over refreshments, daily newspapers are thoughtfully provided.

Open 9am to 5pm Monday to Saturday and 10am to 5pm on Sunday. Tel: 01422 845629

About the Area

The valley of the River Calder was one of West Yorkshire's important areas during and after the industrial revolution, a narrow corridor along which the communications by water, by rail and by road encouraged the development of large numbers of textile mills. Hebden Bridge soon became a focal point in this development, its position at the point where Hebden Water joins the River Calder

On Stoodley Pike

allowing a little more valley bottom space into which mills and the ancillary housing and commerce could be squeezed. There was never enough space, as can be seen from the built up steep valley sides, where 'double decker' terraces of houses cling precariously.

The past and the present combine to make Hebden a place of more than usual interest. The Rochdale Canal (ref. walk no. 17, Todmorden and Lumbutts) is a particular feature, with environmental upgrading in progress and a good riverside park alongside. Cruises are available. Present-day attractions include a cinema, the 'Little Theatre', the craft workshops at Bridge Mill and a Tourist Information Centre.

Stoodley Pike can be seen for miles around, sitting on the edge of high moorland, steep on the Calder side, close to the summit at 402m (1319ft.). The Pike is a huge obelisk built in 1856 to replace a tower, blown down a few years earlier, which had been constructed in 1815 as a thanks offering for peace. There is an internal staircase leading to a viewing balcony. The Pennine Way passes the Pike; a little of the Way is included in the present route.

Hebden Bridge railway station has services on routes connecting Leeds with Manchester and with Burnley, Blackburn, Preston and Blackpool.

The Walk

Walk down the exit roadway from the car park, with a mill building to the left. Turn left at Albert Street to go to the main road. Turn right, pass the cinema and a road junction by the TIC, then cross the road bridge and continue along Market Street for about 200 metres. Turn left at the far side of the Co-operative supermarket at Hebble End.

1. Cross the river, rise over the canal and turn right to follow New Road, signposted to Horsehold. The climb now commences in earnest, half a mile at an unremittingly steep gradient. The hillside is partly wooded, with abundant silver birch. The road is very quiet and the views improve all the time. *Just as the slope eases, go through a signposted gate on the right and walk for 40 metres to a seat at a noted viewpoint. The valley is set out below; Heptonstall is the hilltop village opposite.*

2. After this diversion, continue along the road, now on the original cobbles. As the road bends to the left to Horsehold hamlet, go straight on through a signposted gate, 'Public bridleway, Horsehold Wood', a broad, easy track along the top of the wood. Go straight on at a gate/squeezer stile. In a little more than a quarter of a mile from leaving the road, in a pleasant little wooded valley, fork left, uphill, to avoid crossing the stream, at a signpost 'Kilnshaw Lane and Stoodley Pike'.
   The path is now a little rough and less well defined. Keep the stream close on the right, along the woodland edge, bearing a little left, rising. A short distance before a wall, turn right at an unmarked post to cross the minute stream on a plank to a waymarked post on the far side. Go to a squeezer stile in 20 metres to gain access to a walled grass lane, Pinnacle Lane.

3. Turn right; Stoodley Pike now dominates the view ahead. Closer at hand the upland farming landscape reveals a very limited amount of 'improved' grassland., wrestled over the years from the harsh moor. Bend left, then right, go through a gate and continue. Go over a stile in the wall ahead to head straight for the Pike. Go through a little gate and on to a farm access lane. Turn left to walk past Kershaw Farm to a 'T' junction with Kilnshaw Lane.

4. Turn right to go to Swillington Farm, last farm before the moor and an extreme example of hard upland farming — a few sheep and no evident improved land. Go through a gate to reach the rough moorland, with two signposts ahead. Join the Pennine Way at the first and go left at the second, signposted 'Stoodley Pike', along a track worn by the boots of the famous, A. Wainwright included, and by even more of the less famous. It has to be said that Wainwright didn't particularly enjoy his trek along the Way but was sufficiently magnanimous to pay for a glass of beer at the

northern end for all those who completed the Way, for a period of many years afterwards.

After the slope eases, reach a wall and go over a ladder stile.

5. *A left turn here, assuming fatigue and/or bad weather, heads for home, missing out the Pike.*

    Turn right, go through a squeezer stile in a few metres and walk to the Pike.

6. After relishing the fine views, possibly from the balcony, return by the same route to the ladder stile (*5.*). Do not go over, but continue with the wall on the left to head for Sunderland Pasture, a drab conifer plantation. At the near edge of the Pasture bear left along a very wide lane, presumably an old drove way to and from the moor, Dick's Lane, between walls. Go through a gate to continue. As the lane ends, turn left at a signpost, for 'Rake Head' and go along a clear track.

7. Bear right at a junction, with a wall on the left. As the path more or less peters out, turn left at a gate/stile along a level, walled, lane, still maintaining a good altitude. Pass Rake Head Farm, another sparse upland holding, then a long disused quarry on the right, now really descending, soon in a cutting. Heptonstall is well seen. Reach a surfaced road, but turn right at once, through a gate.

8. Go along a walled lane, turning left, downhill, in about 70 metres along another walled lane, now with an old cobbled surface. At a junction at the bottom go straight on into a rather overgrown grass lane, still descending steeply between the bramble. Go under an odd little bridge and continue. As Crow Nest Wood is reached the path improves, bearing left down a sunken track, then zig zagging down through the wood.

9. At a junction just above a broken wall, turn left to pass behind houses, the path becoming hard surfaced. Reach a residential road; turn left, passing traffic lights and crossing a bridge over the railway line. In a further 40 metres turn right at a 'public footpath' sign and go down a few steps to a cobbled lane. Go left, down the steps, to a bridge over a sluice.

10. Turn right by the canal side footpath, crossing the river and reaching a lock. Cross the bridge over the canal, go to the left of Hebden Bridge Little Theatre, and turn right to walk to the main road in 100 metres. Go across at the traffic lights and follow the road, Bridge Gate, towards 'Haworth and Keighley' to reach the tea/coffee shop in 120 metres, on the left.

After refreshment, turn left, then right at St. George's Square. Cross Crown Street and Albert Street to go straight on into Garden Street for the car park.

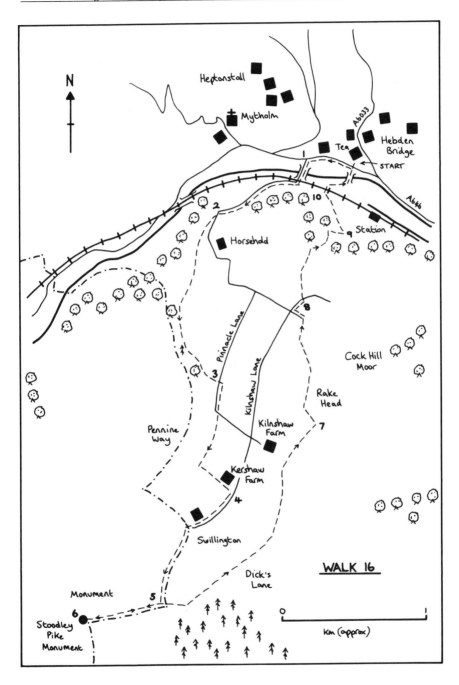

17. Todmorden and Lumbutts

Summary: An excellent walk, including agricultural land high up the side of the Calder Valley, the hamlets of Mankinholes and Lumbutts, the ever interesting town of Todmorden and a return along the towpath of the Rochdale Canal. All on good lanes and footpaths, including part of the Calderdale Way and almost half a mile along a minor upland road. There is a steep climb initially and there are plenty of stiles.

Length: 5 miles (8km)

Car Parking: Small roadside picnic area and car park a little more than one mile east of Todmorden on the A646 main road to Halifax. Grid reference 956247.

Maps: Ordnance Survey Outdoor Leisure 21, South Pennines, 1:25,000. Ordnance Survey Landranger 103, Blackburn and Burnley, 1:50,000.

The Tea Shop

The Craft Centre and Tea Room is situated by the Rochdale Canal. It is not too easy to find but well worth seeking; being popular with local people is usually a good recommendation. Eating indoors one is surrounded by the crafts on display, all for sale. On a good day choose the terrace which has pleasing furniture with sun umbrellas, sitting high above the canal towpath with pleasant views of the canal and the lock. Good quality light meals such as quiche, jacket potatoes, salads, and sandwiches are all available plus tempting cakes and scones for tea. Prices reasonable and service friendly.

Open: 9am to 5pm every day except Christmas Day and Boxing Day. Tel: 01706 818170

About the Area

Todmorden is described in walk no. 18, Todmorden. The present walk gives yet another opportunity to look at the agriculture of the high valley sides of the southern Pennine Hills, just below the true moorland. Bleak, windswept, with climate to match the poverty of the soil, this is an area fit only for sheep and a few cattle, with a patchwork of dark stone walls dividing the meagre land of the steep hillsides. The farm buildings huddle close to the ground, their small windows yielding the least possible amount of whatever warmth and comfort is generated inside. Many of the buildings are obviously of great age, the thick stone walls and heavy stone roofing cover resisting the passage of time. As age, woodworm and rot does eventually take its toll on the original fabric, repairs and renewals are all too often of cheap, temporary material such as corrugated metal.

Pennine farmers are clearly a hardy breed, but the number of abandoned farmsteads bears testimony to those who have given up what appears to be a greatly uneven struggle.

Mankinholes and Lumbutts are small but characterful examples of high Pennine hamlets, apparently growing from the gritstone on which their foundations stand. Mankinholes has a long established youth hostel, whilst Lumbutts has an inn and the 100 ft. tower which housed the water wheel of a former mill.

In the valley, the Rochdale Canal follows the line of the River Calder, an early example (1804) of the establishment of trans-Pennine communication. Like the later (1841) Manchester to Leeds railway line, the construction of the wide canal necessitated great feats of engineering, not perhaps quite so spectacular as the prodigious railway tunnel under the moorland, but nevertheless cumulatively enormously impressive.

Connecting Manchester, Rochdale and the Calder and Hebble Navigation at Sowerby Bridge, the canal is only 33 miles in length, but has no less than 83 locks to cope with the hilly nature of the terrain. In progress is a much-needed major project to regenerate the canal and its surroundings in the Calder Valley.

The Walk

Leave the car park and walk along the roadside pavement towards Todmorden for less than 200 metres, passing a railway viaduct on the right. Turn left at Haugh Road, opposite a 'public footpath' sign on the opposite side of the main road.

1. Cross the bridge over the river and pass a canal lock 'Lobb Mill no.16' to commence the ascent at once, on a surfaced roadway. Immediately after passing a group of dwellings, turn right, up a few old stone steps, to a gate with a 'link path' sign.

   In 10 metres go left at another board 'link path to Calderdale Way' and zig zag steeply up the hillside on a grass path. The extensive view includes the portal of a railway tunnel. After about 200 metres go over a waymarked stile on the left and continue uphill, now with a wall on the right. Stoodley Pike (walk no. 16) is prominent on its hilltop to the left and Todmorden town centre is very much in view below/right.

As the gradient eases, stay with the wall on the right along the edge of pasture. Go over a waymarked stile and bear left, diagonally, across a meadow, being joined by another path from the right, and heading for a waymarked stile and signpost in the left corner. Go over, to head for Mankinholes, keeping close to the wall on the left. Go through an open gateway and continue to a slightly awkward stile in about 50 metres. Proceed along a walled lane to join a minor public road, Cross Lane.

2. Go straight on to Mankinholes, worth a small detour to explore the hamlet; however, our route continues by turning right into a signposted footpath opposite the entrance to the youth hostel.

3. Go over a stile, noting the 'path slippy when wet' warning. Flagged underfoot, the path stays close to the wall on the right, heading straight for Lumbutts. Go over a stile to reach the car parking area by the Top Brinks Inn.

4. Turn left to admire the water wheel tower at close quarters, then sharp right, downhill, on the public road, with the bustle of a former mill race to the left below the road. Stay with this road, Lumbutts Road, which is part of the Calderdale Way, for nearly half a mile, soon rising. Pass the junction with Causeway Wood Road and continue to the near end of an isolated dwelling, Croft Gate. Turn right here at a 'Calderdale Way' waymark.

5. Head for a farm, go through a waymarked gate, and continue along a grass lane between walls. In 150 metres turn left over a stile by a well waymarked post. Walk on with a wall close on the left, rising slightly. Go over a stile by a broken wall and carry on with a wall on the right to a stile in the right corner. Proceed towards a huge farmstead; the views are over Todmorden to a moorland wind farm.
    Go over a waymarked stile at the foot of a slope and follow the worn path to a squeezer stile and a farm roadway.

6. Turn right, over a cattle grid, towards the farm then bear left across the front of the cottages to a waymarked stile. Cross a paddock to another stile in 50 metres and pass through an extensive horse stabling complex. There are waymarks on a post at the far side. Bear left along a farm lane then, at a 'T' junction turn right along a stony surfaced lane, soon bending sharp right to descend towards the church spire, just visible against the trees.

7. The old lane acquires a tarmac surface by a row of cottages, now with a wooded little glen on the right and one really steep section. Descend a hairpin bend by the churchyard, pass a few modern houses and continue down to the church itself. Go left below the churchyard retaining wall and

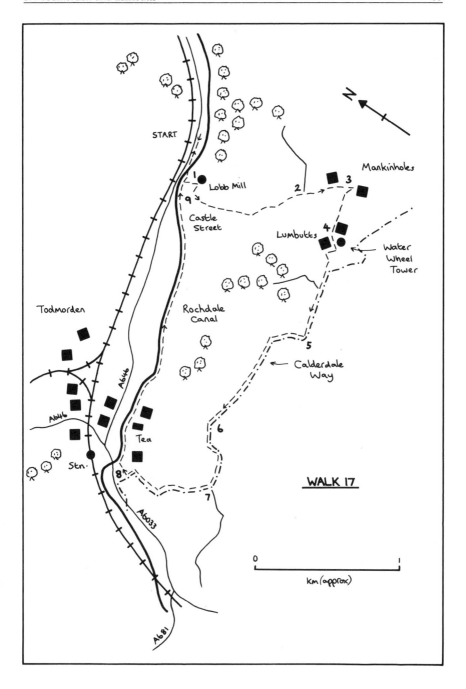

START

1 ● Lobb Mill

9

Castle Street

Mankinholes

2 ■ 3 ■

Lumbutts 4 ■ ■ ●

← Water Wheel Tower

N

Todmorden

Rochdale Canal

5

← Calderdale Way

6

Tea

Stn.

8

7

A646

A646

A6033

A681

WALK 17

0   1

Km (approx)

into Todmorden town centre. Pass across the front of the Golden Lion Inn and walk to the bridge over the Rochdale Canal, at 'Todmorden lock – no. 19'.

8. Cross the bridge and turn left to descend to the towpath. Turn left again to go through the little tunnel under the road. Continue along the towpath for about 150 metres to 'Shop Lock – no. 18'. On the left is Todmorden Craft Centre, with the first floor tea room and terrace.

   After refreshment carry on along the towpath, heading towards Stoodley Pike. Leave the canal by 'Lobb Mill – no. 16' lock.

9. Turn left and then right to retrace the outward route along the roadside to the car park.

The Rochdale Canal, near Todmorden

18. Todmorden

Summary: A well varied walk based on Todmorden, up and over adjacent high ground , between the valleys of the River Calder and Midgelden Brook, with splendid views over the valleys to high moorland. Some woodland, many stiles and a long initial ascent. Paths are generally good; about 1½ miles on surfaced roads.

Length: 5 miles (8km)

Car Parking: Small car park on the railway station approach in Todmorden town centre is recommended. Grid reference 936242.

Maps: Ordnance Survey Outdoor Leisure 21, South Pennines, 1:25,000 Ordnance Survey Landranger 103, Blackburn and Burnley, 1:50,000

The Tea Shop

Situated in the market hall is a smart and stylish cappuccino coffee bar – a branch of the Exchange Coffee Co. This is an ideal venue for coffee – many varieties are offered – tea, orange juice, tea bread crumpets, cakes and ice creams. It is a genuine bar with tall stools and is situated in the centre of the indoor market.

Open: 10am to 4pm on Monday and from Wednesday to Saturday (closed Sunday and Tuesday). Tel: 01706 818558

About the Area

Todmorden is arguably the archetypical Pennine textile town, growing from a nucleus at the strategic point where valleys and their watercourses come together. The tight geography, with steep valley sides rising to high moors, has constrained town expansion, resulting in a close knit community. The only uncertainty over the years has been the administrative difficulty of the Lancashire/Yorkshire boundary passing through the middle of the town, straight through the town hall in fact! A local government reorganisation in 1888 solved this knotty problem and Todmorden has since been very firmly part of West Yorkshire.

Civic pride from the Victorian era onwards has certainly been a great feature. The town hall is quite magnificent for a small town

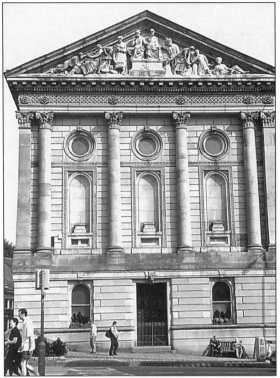
Todmorden Town Hall

and is now open for guided tours several times each year. Equally, Centre Vale Park, opened in 1912, is a showpiece of municipal enterprise, with a Toy and Model Museum and with a sports centre recently constructed alongside.

Noteworthy among the local celebrities of the industrial revolution were the Fielden family, particularly John, who managed the family business for many years from 1811, introducing steam power for the first time to one of the family mills in 1818. He became a Member of Parliament, using his wealth and influence largely for the benefit of the town and his own employees. He was much involved in workers' welfare movements and was highly regarded by the great reformer, Lord Salisbury.

The town's churches have a curious history. The older St. Mary's Church closed when Christ Church opened in 1832, reopening in 1860 in 'opposition' to the newer church. It was then found that the legal rights had never been transferred to Christ Church and that marriages conducted there for 30 years were not, in fact, legal. The Fielden family, like much of the local population, were fiercely non-conformist. The Unitarian Church which they built and paid for in 1869 is in a Gothic revival style with a high spire and an overall grandeur very rare in non-conformist places of worship.

Dobroyd Castle was built by one of John Fielden's sons as a magnificent family home in 1866. It is now used as a Buddhist retreat. The very ancient Todmorden Hall is in private ownership.

Yet another feature of this fascinating market town is the Rochdale Canal, described more fully in walk no. 17, Todmorden and Lumbutts.

The railway station has services within the West Yorkshire Metro system on the line from Manchester to Leeds.

The Walk

Leave the railway station car parking area and turn right, down a flight of steps. At the main road, opposite the town hall, turn left along the Burnley road to pass under the railway viaduct. Pass the bus station and the former cinema, which has an impressive, now rather neglected, facade. Pass Todmorden Cricket Club, then turn left into Centre Vale Park

1. Pass public conveniences on the left and continue along a tarmac footpath to the woodland at the top of the park. Rise along a broad, unsurfaced, track, turning left at a junction. The pleasant woodland includes plenty of rhododendron. Pass above the large, now redundant, Christ Church and then turn sharp right at once to ascend a steep, cobbled, path, presumably an old mill workers'(or packhorse?) route. Go straight across at a junction by a seat to continue the steep ascent, taking care if the surface is greasy. At the top is a seat and a few steps up to a minor public road.

2. Cross the road and go up a few more steps to a gate with a 'public footpath' sign. Walk up the field, initially on a path in a shallow depression, then stay close to the fence on the left for easy walking over grass to the field corner, with two stiles. Go through that on the left, to head by the side of a wall for a clump of trees. Bear right, then go to the left through a little gate.

Carry on with a fence on the left, ascending over meadow grass. Go over the stone wall by a stile at the top. Below is Dobroyd Castle, now in view. Turn left by the side of the wall to head for a farm, Ping Hold, barely 100 metres away. We are now on the Calderdale Way. Go over a waymarked stile beside a gate and then along a farm access track. There is a small rock outcrop to the right and a substantial symmetrical building, with the appearance of a former municipal hospital, below to the left.

Go through/over a gate/stile and turn right, then left, to pass behind Stones House, a fine building in a splendid position. Next is a great 'surprise view' of the high moorland on the far side of the valley of the Midgelden Brook and Gorpley Clough. Go over a stile to join a narrow little road, Stones Lane.

3. Turn right to walk for about a half mile along this quiet byway, passing two large standing stones then Stones Grange Farm. About 150 metres after the farm, turn left through a gate at a bridleway sign. A good path heads straight for Moor Hey Farm. Go through a gate, then another gate, then between walls to a third gate and over a cobbled surface by the farm to another minor road.

Turn right, uphill, along the roadside. At a 'T' junction by the Dog and Partridge Inn, follow a 'public footpath' sign, crossing a cattle grid and then go along a wide, stony, track.

4. *From the inn a short cut can be taken by turning right and walking by the roadside for nearly half a mile to the farmstead at Todmorden Edge.*

On the main route stay with the track, passing a small disused quarry on the left. There are good views across to the high land to the north of Todmorden. Just before the next farm, West End, cut across to the right, through grass and rushes, to a waymarked stile. Go over and descend gently along an old lane between walls. Go over a stile and leave the old lane by turning right, over another stile, at once. Follow a sunken lane for 150 metres or so and then sweep round to the left at a 'Todmorden Centenary Way' waymark on a post near the issue of a tiny spring. This section of the route has particularly good views over Todmorden, including Stoodley Pike.

On reaching Flail Croft Farm the path stays by the fence up to the right, above the farm, through a decrepit gate, then by a green track to join the farm access roadway, uphill to Todmorden Edge Farm. At the far end of the buildings, turn left down a walled lane with a rough grass surface at a 'Calderdale Way' signpost.

5. Go through/over a gate/stile at the bottom of the lane, to continue along a grass path by a wall and through a well waymarked kissing gate. The path descends steeply through Buckley Wood, with spectacular views through the trees. Go down a few steps to join a roadway, turning left for 100 metres, then sharp right at a 'Calderdale Way link path' signpost.

6. Continue down a broad track. Just after a wide cleared area, with seats, fork left to carry on the descent. Fork left again in 40 metres. From here, any route across the park will suffice to return to the Burnley road. A good path stays above the open parkland to reach a junction used in the outward part of the walk. Turn left at that junction to retrace the route past the public conveniences and along the road to the town centre. The market and tea shop are to the left after passing under the railway viaduct.

7. From the market, turn left, cross the road and go back up the steps to the car park.

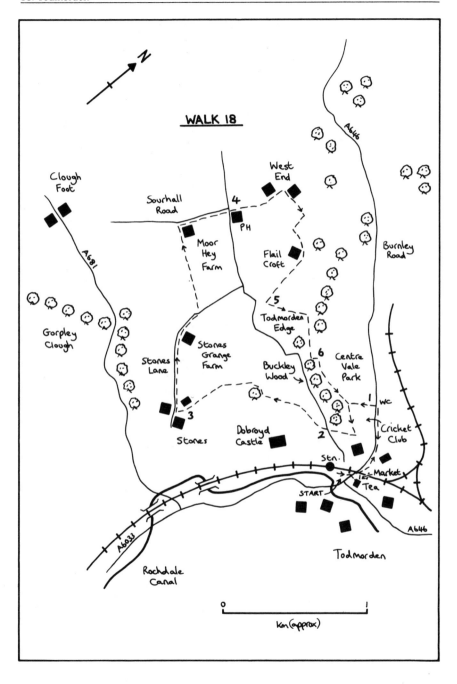

WALK 18

19. Shibden Hall

Summary: An interesting walk through countryside just outside Halifax, based on the extensive park surrounding Shibden Hall. There is a fair amount of ascent, notably at the start of the walk. First-rate underfoot, including a short length of minor road. Several stiles, none of which is difficult.

Length: 3¾ miles (6km)

Car Parking: The lower car park, close to the lake, in Shibden Park. The park is signposted from the A58, Halifax to Bradford and Leeds road. Grid reference 109260. (Do not follow signs for the 'Hall')

Maps: Ordnance Survey Pathfinder 691, Halifax, 1:25,000. Ordnance Survey Landranger 104, Leeds and Bradford, 1:50,000.

The Tea Shop

The tea room at Shibden Hall is a pleasant venue. It is furnished with pine tables and chairs; photographs of Shibden in times long gone adorn the walls. Outside is a peaceful, sheltered terrace – an excellent place to enjoy tea. Super menu here; the sandwiches are made to order and of good quality – those sampled included, tuna and cucumber, a cheese and ham toastie, and toasted corned beef with onion. Toasted fruit tea-cakes were served with plenty of butter and jam. Cakes available included Yorkshire sticky parkin. Service noticeably pleasant and prices most reasonable.

Open: 11am to 4pm from Monday to Saturday and 12pm to 5pm on Sundays from early March to the end of November. During December, January, and February open only on Saturdays and Sundays. Tel: 01422 359454 ext. 257

About the Area

The fine visitor attraction of Shibden Hall and its park is owned and managed by Calderdale Council. The part timber framed building, originally 15th century with later additions, has a long and varied history. The interior is oak panelled and the furnishings are rich and atmospheric.

The Hall is open every day during the season (afternoon only on

Shibden Hall

Sundays). Winter opening is more restricted; tel. 01422 532246 for information. The park has lake, miniature railway, pitch and putt, children's amusements and a programme of events on high season Sundays. There are also refreshment kiosks.

Halifax town centre is less than 1½ miles (2km) away, reached by a variety of bus routes. In this predominantly textile town, The Piece Hall is a fine historic building complemented by an extensive modern shopping centre.

The walk is largely through the Southowram area, which has a history of stone quarrying/mining, with the odd coal mine.

The Walk

Leave the car park by the vehicular entrance and bear left, keeping to the right of the lake, along a surfaced roadway. The lake attracts a fair number of waterfowl, principally mallard. Pass a catering kiosk and bear right, uphill, to the childrens' playground. Go left in 30 metres to pass public conveniences and head for the tunnel under the railway line.

1. After the tunnel follow an old paved footpath rising through farmland. Go through a little gate then, at the top of this section, through a second gate to reach a public road; there is a farmhouse to the right here. Go across and into a modern residential estate at Shibden Hall Croft., still rising. Turn right then left and then bear left into an old lane, Pump Lane, initially over grass.

2. After bearing right, the lane rises quite steeply between well spaced stone walls. As height is gained, long views open up to the left, towards Hipperholme, across the valley of the Red Beck. To the right are two stubby stone towers, one at least apparently being a ventilation shaft for the railway tunnel under Beacon Hill. Reach a wide track and go almost straight across to a narrow footpath between walls. The path is now level, a little overgrown. Go through an old squeezer stile, then slightly downhill to a tiny zigzag and continue to a curiously arranged squeezer stile to surmount a stone wall. Rise diagonally across a small field, largely on old paving stones, and go through another stile.

3. Turn right immediately to pass along the end of a terrace of cottages in Marsh Delves hamlet. Join a public road and turn left to walk to a 'T' junction. Turn left at the junction and then leave the surfaced road to take a wide, level, unsurfaced roadway, forking to the right and reaching Marsh Farm in 100 metres.

   Pass between Marsh Farm and Marshfields House to continue along a straight lane ahead, slightly downhill

4. Keep straight on at a junction, with an operational quarry to the right. Turn left at the bottom and carry on the descent to a 'T' junction by a ruinous farmhouse. Turn right, downhill.

   At the next 'T' junction a left turn for 30 metres leads to a stone pedestal with a plaque giving information about the Magna Via, the ancient road from Halifax to the east, of which this lane is part, and also 'Wakefield Gate', Dark Lane and Hollow Way.

   Resume the circuit, downhill on a broad lane which becomes Norcliffe Lane at a terrace of cottages.

5. Cross the bridge over Red Beck and turn left at a 'public footpath Shibden Hall Road' sign. The path, initially by the side of the stream, is minor but clear enough on the ground. Go over a stile in a few metres and cross rough grassland, bristling with thistles. Go over another stile and continue through coppiced woodland. Approach a modern house and turn right to ascend a few old stone steps to Shibden Hall Road.

6. Turn left, downhill, to walk along the roadside. Opposite Shibden Hall Croft turn right, through the little gate, to retrace the outward route down into Shibden Park. After passing through the tunnel, turn left through the children's playground, to follow a broad gravel track, uphill through woodland. Bear right to pass a lily pond and reach the side of the Hall. Go left, up steps, to the terrace below the tea room.

7. From the Hall go straight down the grass back towards the lake, bearing left after passing the end of a tree belt to reach the car park.

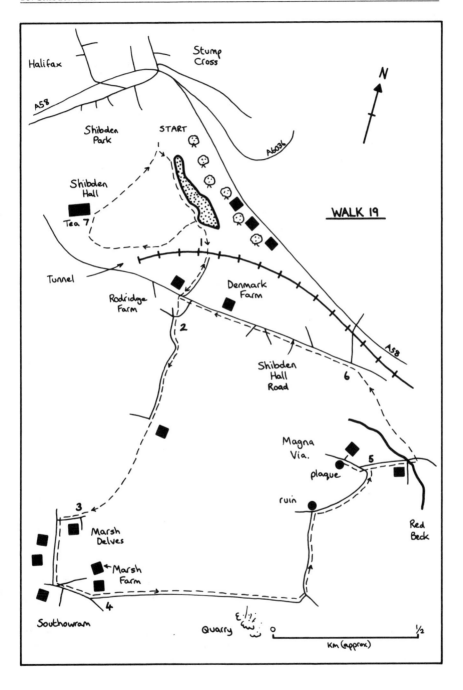

Halifax

Stump Cross

A58

Shibden Park

START

Shibden Hall

Tea 7

Tunnel

Rodridge Farm

Denmark Farm

N

A6036

WALK 19

1

2

A58

Shibden Hall Road

6

Magna Via.

plaque

ruin

5

Red Beck

3

Marsh Delves

Marsh Farm

4

Southowram

Quarry

Km (approx)

½

20. Marsden and the Moor

Summary: Although not a long walk, this circuit gives a real taste of high Pennine moorland, coupled with some agricultural land and the towpath of the Huddersfield Narrow Canal. There is an ascent of several hundred feet to reach top moor level but nowhere is this steep or difficult underfoot. Generally good paths with less than 10 stiles in total.

Length: 6½ miles (10.4km)

Car Parking: Several possibilities in Marsden. The railway station is very convenient for this walk. Grid reference 046118.

Maps: Ordnance Survey Outdoor Leisure 21, South Pennines (part), 1:25,000. Ordnance Survey Pathfinder 714, Holmfirth and Saddleworth Moor, (part) 1:25,000. Ordnance Survey Landranger 110, Sheffield and Huddersfield, 1:50,000.

The Tea Shop

The tea shop at Pennine Wholefoods in the centre of Marsden is well worth patronising. Furniture is plain and sturdy; the work by local artists displayed on the walls is available to purchase. Good selection of food including the robust 'Pennine' breakfast which is available throughout the day and may well be appreciated on a cold, rainy afternoon. Cakes are made on the premises – the date flapjack is highly recommended whilst the lemon cake was tangy, moist, and utterly delicious.

Open: 9.30am to 4pm from Monday to Saturday and 10am to 3.30pm on Sundays. Please note that closing times could vary depending on the weather – do check by 'phone if in any doubt. Tel: 01484 847715

About the Area

Marsden is a gritty, no nonsense, but not unattractive little town at the head of the Colne Valley, the last Yorkshire outpost before the high moorland which separates Yorkshire from Lancashire, just a few miles over the top. The town has the characteristics of the early years of the industrial revolution, when mill builders pushed higher and higher up the valleys to utilise, both for power and for various textile processes, the fast flowing water which pours from the soggy moors in such quantity.

Trans Pennine communications have inevitably made full use of valleys like the Colne. In packhorse days, bridges were constructed across the rivers and major streams; Marsden has surviving examples at Closegate and in the town centre. Next, in 1811, came the Huddersfield Narrow Canal, an amazing feat of engineering with the Standedge Tunnel, at 3 miles 135 yards, the longest in the United Kingdom; it is also the highest above sea level. It was closed in 1944 but is about to be renovated and re-opened. In 1846-49 the railway followed, with a tunnel of the same name, later to become three tunnels as traffic increased. Boats and trains both disappear into the bowels of the earth at Tunnel End, a little way above Marsden, on the line of this walk. Most recent in the concentration of communications along the Colne is the main road, the A62, Manchester to Huddersfield, which climbs out of the valley at Marsden to cross over Standedge.

Marsden Moor is a high, windswept, place grazed by hardy sheep, with the wild beauty which is so appreciated by Pennine walkers. A large part of the moor comprises the Marsden Moor Estate, in the care of the National Trust.

Above Marsden

The Walk

From the car parking by the railway station walk along the adjacent canal towpath as far as its termination at Tunnel End. Close to Tunnel End there are small picnic areas beside a track which is close on the left of the towpath.

1. At Tunnel End cross over the canal on a bridge. The long-term renovation works have necessitated a small footpath diversion here, but the route is waymarked and easy to follow. It rises to the left along a little path leading to a gap in a wall and a few steps, followed by a rather high stile on to a minor road. *The stile can be avoided by walking along the road from Tunnel End to an inn and then turning very sharp left.* Turn left along the minor road, soon rising to join the main road. Turn left along the roadside pavement for about 350 metres, passing a long terrace of houses on the right.

2. Cross over the road to a footpath at the far end of the terrace. Go up a few steps and continue uphill, between walls. Go over two stiles and carry on uphill, with a wall on the left. At a junction keep straight on towards a farm, walking over grass to a stile. Keep to the left of the farmhouse and head for a surfaced access road, climbing towards the next farm.
At a signpost by a stile and gate bear left to 'Mount Road'.

3. The excellent wide track is now part of the 'Standedge Trail', across the flank of Pule Hill and with good views over Butterley Reservoir. Below left, on the fringe of Marsden, is a classic example of a mill community. Join Old Mount Road and go right to join the main road in 50 metres.

4. Turn right and, in 30 metres, cross the road to an upright stone and go steeply down the bank on a little path which needs care in wet weather. Cross a stream on a plank bridge and climb the far bank on a similar path. Pass an 'ST' waymark on a post. The path now goes on across the moor for about 1 mile, good walking on springy grass, with Redbrook Reservoir coming into view to the right and Pule Hill quite impressive on the far side of the road. Immediately before a stream feeding into the reservoir is reached, the obvious stone-surfaced path leads across the stream and descends to the right.

5. Ignore this, going straight on, then left on what at first seems to be a more minor path, soon helped by a few steps and then rising along stone paving. This is now part of the hallowed Pennine Way, soon reaching the boundary of the National Trust Marsden Moor Estate at a ladder stile.
Continue through an area with much exposed peat and shortly leave the Estate at another ladder stile. At a junction of paths 150 metres or so before Black Moor Reservoir, turn left. Bear right by a waymark on a post to cross the reservoir dam. There is a mini sandy beach in one corner.

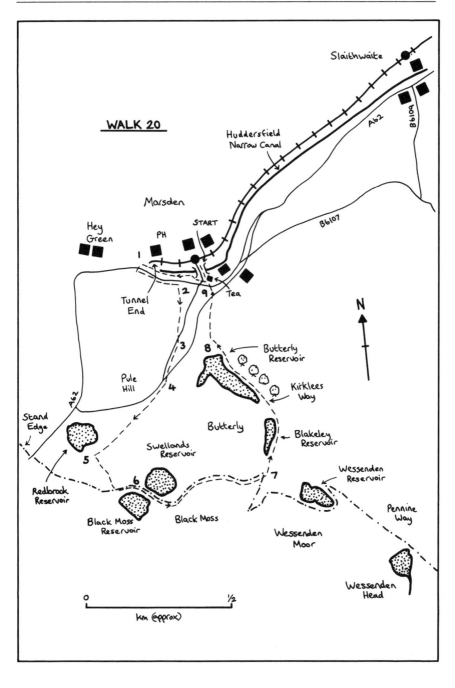

WALK 20

6. The water below to the left is Swelland Reservoir. Continue across the moor on a flagged way, soon commencing a long, steady, descent, with Wessenden Reservoir coming into view. Cross a stream, slightly awkward, and continue to a small waterworks structure, where the path forks.

7. Go left here, steeply downhill on a narrow path, heading for a footbridge over the large stream at the bottom. Cross over and ascend the far bank bearing left to join the Kirklees Way which runs along the top. *Alternatively, a track to the left which stays at a lower level makes a fine route, terraced along the side of the valley, but this is apparently not a right of way, as the gate at the far end must be climbed to join the Kirklees Way.* In either case, turn left along the Way to walk past Blakeley and Butterley Reservoirs. Don't miss a small wooden sculpture on the right, opposite the top end of Butterley Reservoir.

Just beyond the dam of the latter reservoir, join a minor road and turn left at once, through a gate and down an interminable flight of steps, with a lovely bank of heather to the right.

8. Follow the signpost at the bottom, bearing right along a broad, easy, track fringed by bramble. The route goes to and through a large mill before joining the public highway.

Turn left, downhill, to reach a road junction at a roundabout. Go straight ahead, fork left under a road tunnel, then bear round to the right to the main street. The tea shop is a little way further, in the Market Place.

9. To return to the car parking area, walk back along the main street, cross the river on the road bridge and continue uphill directly to the railway station.

21. Slaithwaite

Summary: This circular walk within the Colne Valley combines the canal tow path with a section of the officially designated Colne Valley Circular Walk The latter, largely crossing agricultural land, is sufficiently high on the valley side to provide good long views across and along the valley. There is a short but quite steep ascent of the main valley side and a lesser ascent of the Bradley Brook valley side. Not all sections of the footpaths are entirely clear on the ground and there is one partial obstruction, but no real problems. Many stiles.

Length: 4 miles (6.4km)

Car Parking: Free parking area for about 15 vehicles near the lock which is at the stopped end of the waterway. Approaching from the main by-passing road (A62) and by the main street, after crossing the river turn left, then left again at once. Grid reference 078140.

Maps: Ordnance Survey Outdoor Leisure 21, South Pennines, 1:25,000 Ordnance Survey Landranger 110, Sheffield and Huddersfield, 1:50,000.

The Tea Shop

Finding the Floating Tea Room on the Huddersfield Narrow Canal in Slaithwaite was a complete surprise – just one of the many delights on these walks. The menu is incredibly comprehensive and especially impressive when one sees the cramped surroundings of the galley. Dishes produced include soup, salads, sandwiches and toasties, homemade cakes (yes, made in the galley!), ice creams, and a variety of drinks from Coca Cola to creamy hot chocolate. A visit to this unique venue should not be missed. In fine weather, outside tables supplement the limited internal space.

Open: 10am to 6pm from 1st April to 30th September every day except Mondays and from 10am to 4pm from 1st October to 31st March but closed on Mondays and Tuesdays during the winter months. Please note open on all Bank Holidays except Christmas Day and Boxing Day. Tel: 01484 846370

Slaithwaite Tea Barge

About the Area

Slaithwaite (locally 'Slawit') is the next community in the Colne Valley downstream from Marsden, and is another focal point in the development of the textile industry, now more diversified in Slaithwaite. There are shops, inns and other facilities as would be expected in a small town.

Inevitably the narrow valley bottom has provided the route for the successive communications, the canal being followed by the railway and the A62 main road. There is still a railway service on the Manchester to Huddersfield line.

The Huddersfield Narrow Canal certainly adds interest to the town centre, its towpath providing both a favourite local stroll, and the pleasant connecting link for this walk. A length of almost half a mile of the canal has been filled in for many years, but is obviously ready for restoration as part of the overall scheme for this canal. It is not too difficult to trace the former route on the ground.

Situated further from the high Pennine moors than Marsden, the immediate surroundings of the town are less severe, but there is Black Moor to the south and much of the local agriculture is very much moorland fringe.

The Walk

Turn left from the car park and walk away from the canal lock towards the town centre, preferably along the line obviously intended for the canal restoration, beside the River Colne to a major road junction. Cross the road, keep to the left of a restaurant and continue through a car park across the front of a mill.

1. Carry on along a surfaced footpath in a linear green area, still on the likely route for the new section of canal. Cross a little road and take a narrow footpath opposite, clearly a remnant of the old canal towpath, soon reaching the remains of a lock and the towpath proper. Walk along this section of the towpath for a little less than half a mile; there is one more lock before Lees Mill, dated 1855, is reached, close by a bridge.

2. Turn right here, go through a mill area, turn left to cross the River Colne on a modern road bridge, then right to head for the main road. Go straight across the road to a 'public footpath' sign and follow a surfaced garage access drive. In 25 metres turn right up a few steps, by a signpost with a 'CVCW' waymark. The path over grass is narrow but adequate, climbing steadily and passing a waymark on a gatepost.The path becomes a lane as a hamlet is reached.

3. A short distance before a rather incongruous brick built estate, turn right along a minor path, keeping close to an old stone wall on the right, to rudimentary steps, stile, and waymark, a frequent combination along this section of the walk. After another waymark the path becomes an excellent grass terrace giving grandstand views of the Colne Valley, with Slaithwaite dominant.
   On reaching Heywoods Farm, the route keeps to the right of the buildings; there are little steps at a waymarked left turn. Descend along the unsurfaced farm access roadway to a minor road.

4. Walk downhill for 40 metres to a 'Lower Hey' footpath sign and turn left. Go up steps, keeping above the wall on the right. Go over a rudimentary stile and continue; the path is just about visible on the grass. There is a stile with two steps before passing very close to the front of dwellings, to a little gate at the far end of the garden.
   Descend to the bottom of the valley, Kitchen Clough, bearing to the right to head for a terrace of tall houses. Go over a stile, cross the stream on a little bridge, over another stile, then up a short, sharp, rise towards a public road; there is a wall close on the left. Go over a stile at the top and then right to reach the road.

5. Turn left along the roadside pavement for 40 metres, cross then turn right at a 'public footpath' signpost to take a grassy uphill track. Go right, then

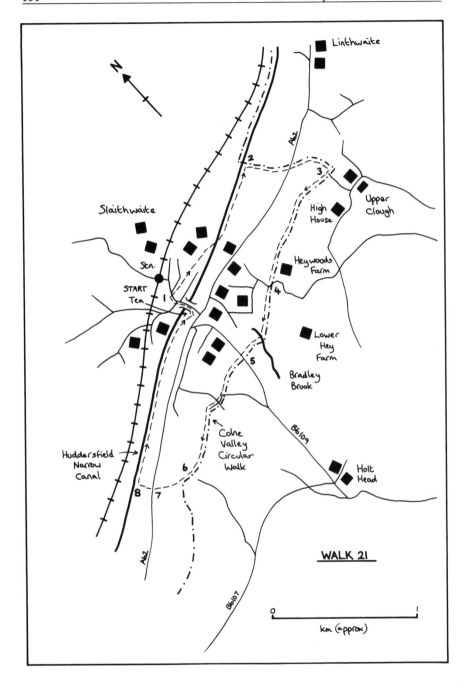

WALK 21

left, to follow a waymark on a post, making for a stile at the top. Stay above a wall to head for a farm and go over a stone stile to a minor road. Turn right, then left along the road, through the attractive hamlet of New House.

Go across a junction, then turn left in 20 metres along a waymarked stony track between buildings. Go round the end of a gate to follow a grass track, passing a waymark on a high post. The Colne Valley views are still splendid, now rather more rural than before. As the track forks, stay above the wall, until a gap with stone steps is reached. Go over two more stiles as the gentle descent continues towards the chapel at Hill Top.

6. Reach the public road and turn right for 30 metres and then left into Hollins Lane. In 100 metres turn right, over a waymarked stile to descend to the valley bottom. The little used path soon bends a little to the left to continue between broken stone walls and over several stiles; take care with the semi-concealed large stones underfoot. Reach the main road down steps at the bottom.

7. Cross the road to a gap in the opposite wall with a 'public footpath' sign, leading straight into a smallholding. Bear right then left through the small-holding to a gap in the far boundary fence. Turn left here to walk to a post with waymarks, turning sharp right by the post to descend the bank on a terraced footpath leading to a footbridge over the River Colne.

8. Go over a stile and cross the bridge to reach the canal towpath beside a lock. Turn right to return to Slaithwaite. The canal hereabouts is attrac-tively rural with virtually no evidence that this is an industrial valley. After passing another lock, the church tower and the chimney of Upper Mill soon come into view. The lock by the mill has a 'guillotine' bottom gate and a boat-launching ramp. The 'Moonraker' tea barge is just a little fur-ther. After refreshments, cross the adjacent canal bridge by the lock to return to the car park.

22. Holmfirth and Underbank

Summary: A largely urban walk through and then along the fringe of Holmfirth, mainly on hard surfaces. As the town is squeezed into steep sided valleys, there is a fair amount of up and down, including a prolonged ascent at the outset. No stiles or other impediments.

Length: 2½ miles (4km)

Car Parking: Several public car parks in the town centre. The pay and display car park adjacent to the Pioneer supermarket is spacious and convenient. Grid reference 146086.

Maps: Ordnance Survey Outdoor Leisure 1, The Dark Peak, 1:25,000. Ordnance Survey Pathfinder 714, Huddersfield and Marsden, 1:25,000. Ordnance Survey Landranger 110, Sheffield and Huddersfield, 1:50,000.

The Tea Shop

Popular Holmfirth has many places to eat. The tea shop chosen for this walk is the Penny Lane Pantry. Housed in a large building, tea rooms can be found on two floors and every room has bric-a-brac displayed for sale, so there is plenty to look at whilst waiting for the chosen refreshments to be served. Extensive menu with dish of the day chalked on the blackboard. For tea try such traditional items as muffins, cinnamon toast, and Yorkshire fat rascals; super selection of scones such as orange and sultana, apple and cinnamon, cheese, and others. An inclusive cream tea or the afternoon tea with sandwiches offer good value. If tempted by high tea, savouries such as sausage, egg and chips, bacon grill, or a salad are all available. Good quality tea and coffee served in china cups of varied designs.

Open: 10am to 4pm (open later in the summer months) everyday all the year except Christmas Day and Boxing Day. Tel: 01484 688151.

About the Area

The textile town of Holmfirth is squeezed into the steep sided valleys of the River Holme and its tributary the Ribbleden stream. So much so that many of the buildings, particularly terraced cottages, have been built on what seem to be impossible slopes, clinging to the

Holmfirth: Sid's Café

hillside with three or even four storeys on the lower side and two storeys on the upper side. Many of these terraces have one dwelling occupying the lower two floors, with a completely separate dwelling occupying the two upper floors – a 'flying freehold'. The respective front (and only) doors are at levels one and three, in different streets, facing in opposite directions. There is, of course, no back yard or garden space, hence the lines of washing in front of the houses. The overall effect, with flights of steps and steep, winding, narrow streets and alleys – 'ginnels'- is highly characteristic and quite fascinating.

The rapid local expansion of textile mills and associated cottages early in the 19th century resulted in the development of peripheral areas such as Underbank, using the water of the Ribbleden stream for powering the mills and for textile processing.

The abundance of water has, however, been a mixed blessing to Holmfirth. Great floods have swept along the valley, notably in 1777 and in 1852 when the Bilberry Reservoir burst its banks and the resultant flood drowned 81 people. The remarkable depth of the water in the town centre is recorded on plaques on the town bridge and on the Napoleonic memorial near the bus station.

No one can visit Holmfirth without being very quickly made aware that the town and its surroundings have provided the locations for filming the television series 'Last of the Summer Wine' since its inception in 1971. Love it or hate it, you can't avoid it in Holmfirth. Sid's Café, The Wrinkled Stocking Tea Room, Compo's Restaurant, mini-bus tours and an exhibition open daily, all combine to attract hordes of visitors from far and wide, no doubt doing wonders for the local economy.

Quite apart from the industrial history, the interest of the buildings and the 'Summer Wine' overlay, the town centre is well provided with facilities such as shops, inns, market hall, cinema, craft centres, postcard museum and a tourist information centre. The parish church of the Holy Trinity, a replacement for a church damaged in the 1777 flood, is Georgian, with an interior gallery.

The upper parts of the valley sides, as included in this walk, provide excellent viewpoints from which the town and its satellite settlements can be appreciated.

The Walk

From the Pioneer car park head towards the town centre by crossing the river on the footbridge and turning right. Continue by the riverside to the bus station and cross the road to the parish church. Go up the steps to the right of the church, bear left, then go up more steps to reach Bunkers Hill, a tarmac surfaced lane, rising steeply. Join another road and bear left. At the next junction, by Quarry Mount, turn right to continue the steady ascent along a surfaced lane, the gradient reaching 25% in places.

1. Once clear of the dwellings, the views over the Holme Valley are great, including the tower on Castle Hill, close to Huddersfield. On reaching a 'T' junction at Cliff Road, turn sharp right to follow this road for some distance, high up the valley side and almost level.

2. After passing through a tiny hamlet, the road rises and bends to the left. There is a well-placed seat on top of the roadside bank. Turn sharp right, downhill, at New Laithe Lane.

3. In 200 metres turn left at a 'public bridleway' sign to follow a narrow old walled lane, part cobbled. In a further 200 metres or so, just before a sports field, turn right along a similar lane, soon reaching the hamlet of Gulley.

4. Turn right, downhill, on the public road, then left in 15 metres into Gulley Terrace. At a fork, keep right, downhill. On the left at the next junction is

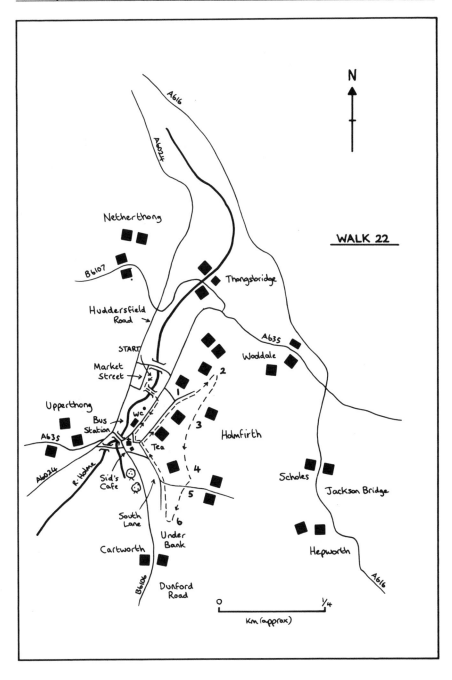

N

A616

A6024

Netherthong

B6107

Thongsbridge

Huddersfield
Road

A635

START

Waddale

Market
Street

Upperthong

Bus
Station

WC

A635

Holmfirth

A6024

R. Holme

Tea

Sid's
Cafe

Scholes

Jackson Bridge

South
Lane

Under
Bank

Cartworth

B6106

Dunford
Road

Hepworth

A616

WALK 22

0   ¼

Km (approx)

Underbank Well, an interesting survival of an early, primitive, public water supply. After the well, turn sharp left up a rising cobbled lane, Well Hill. The track narrows between walls, soon reaching a public road and a wide road junction.

5. Turn sharp right into Upper Bank End Road. At the next road junction turn right, downhill, heading for a mill with chimney. At the base of the chimney turn right, along Underbank Old Road.

6. Until the 1820s construction of the turnpike, the present main B6106 road, this was the route from Holmfirth to the south. Go straight across at a junction to continue the same line, eventually joining South Lane to descend steeply to the town centre, beside the church and close to the tea shop. From the tea shop, return to the car park along the outward route.

23. Holmfirth and Cartworth

Summary: Another short walk based on the little town of Holmfirth and its immediate surroundings. The tracks are good, including quiet roads, with just one section likely to be muddy. Up and down, with a steady ascent of the hillside above Washpit Mill. No stiles.

Length: 3 miles (5km)

Car Parking: Holmfirth town centre. The Pioneer supermarket car park, as detailed for walk no. 22, is convenient. Pay and display.

Maps: Ordnance Survey Pathfinder 714, Holmfirth and Saddleworth Moor, 1:25,000. Ordnance Survey Outdoor Leisure 1, The Peak District, Dark Peak Area (recent double sided editions), 1:25,000. Ordnance Survey Landranger 110, Sheffield and Huddersfield, 1:50,000.

The Tea Shop

This part of West Yorkshire in understandably popular because of 'The Last of the Summer Wine' programmes. We felt that one of the venues for tea in Holmfirth might be 'Sid's Café' which is authentic but very tiny and always full so instead we visited 'The Wrinkled Stocking' which is very evocative of Nora Batty and Compo. Adacent is a small collection of Summer Wine memorabilia (admission charge). The tea room offers a choice of food and drinks including good quality cakes. The 'Holmfirth' cream tea comprises scones, cream and jam whilst the traditional afternoon tea includes sandwiches and cakes. Light meals such as beans on toast or egg on toast are served. Drinks include a choice of blends of tea, coffee, Horlicks, milk shakes, and other cold drinks.

Open: 10am to 5pm everyday (closes at 4.30pm outside main season). Also please note that hours and days may vary in the winter months but always open at weekends. If in any doubt, do telephone first. Tel: 01484 681408

About the Area

Holmfirth is briefly described in walk no. 22. Cartworth has no real nucleus, being just a scattered hamlet with ancient origins situated

The Wrinkled Stocking

on one side of the high tongue of land which separates the Holme and Ribblesden valleys. Before the industrial revolution, the local textile trade was a true cottage industry; hand weavers lived in houses which were often of three storeys, the highest floor being used as a weaving loft. Delivery of raw materials and the dispatch of the finished products to market involved the use of pack horses, hence the large number of old paved and cobbled routes and of pack horse bridges in this area. Many of the hand weavers' houses still stand and can readily be identified. Scenically the highlight of this walk is the fine lane which terraces high above the Holme Valley on the return to Holmfirth.

The Walk

Cross the bridge, turn right and walk by the river to the bus station, as in route 22. Cross to the front of the church, bearing right, then turn left into Dunford Road. Turn left again in 10 metres into South Lane, climbing steeply.

1. After passing a pair of stone semi-detached houses, nos. 44 and 46, fork right, downhill, along Underbank Old Road. Continue to the main Dunford Road.

2. *For a slightly shorter, easier, route you can walk along Dunford Road from the town centre to this point.*
   Go straight across into an unmade track by a telephone box. This is Dover Lane, along the bottom of the Ribbleden Valley, whose little stream formerly powered several mills. The track becomes surfaced as a modern house is passed. Cross a stream and pass older houses before reaching the remains of Dover Mill. The vehicular track ends at

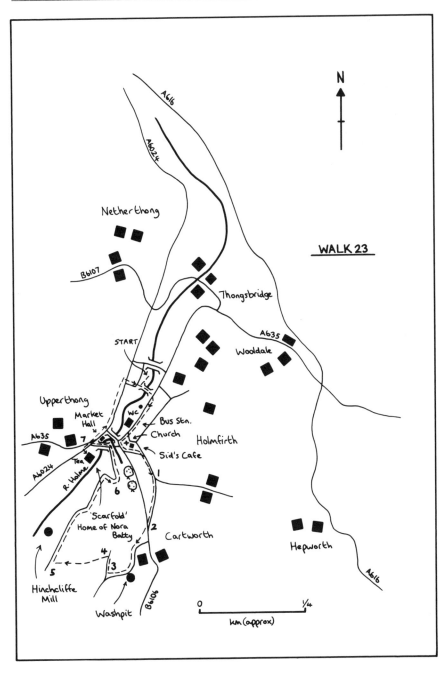

N

WALK 23

A616

A624

Netherthong

B6107

Thongsbridge

A635

START

Wooldale

Upperthong

Market
Hall

WC

7

A635

Bus Stn.

Church

Holmfirth

A624

Tea

Sid's Cafe

R. Holme

6

1

'Scarfold'
Home of Nora
Batty

2

Cartworth

Hepworth

4

A616

5

3

B6106

Hinchcliffe
Mill

Washpit

0   ¼

km (approx)

Ribblebank House. Bear right up a grassy path rising between walls. This section is often muddy.

Join a very minor public road by Washpit Mills (now Westwood Yarns Ltd.) and turn right, steeply uphill; note the survival of part of the old cobbled road surface.

3. At a 'T' junction turn right. The dwelling on the right has a 'Marble Hall' nameplate. At the next road junction there is a seat well placed for views over the Ribbleden Valley.

Turn sharp left into Cartworth Bank Road.

4. Rise gently to cross the high ground between the two valleys, with moorland to the west of Holmfirth and one modern wind turbine, whirling in isolation, now in view. Continue rising to a little stone hamlet, Well Houses, with a former Methodist Chapel.

As the top of this broad plateau is reached, turn right at a crossroads into an unsurfaced lane.

5. The lane forms an excellent high level terrace overlooking the Holme Valley for most of the way back to Holmfirth. To the left is Holme Moss transmitter and to the right, Emley Moor mast. Pass two former quarries on the right and an abandoned farm with some old buildings on the left as the lane descends towards Holmfirth. The tracks bears strongly to the right to join a public road.

6. Turn sharp left to continue the descent, passing a small old school. After the junction with Cemetery Road, our route becomes Rotcher Road, leading down to the town centre. The Wrinkled Stocking Tea Room is found at Scarfold by turning left and crossing the river.

7. Return to the car park by leaving the tea room by the opposite door, on to Huddersfield Road, and turning right. Pass the tourist information centre and the end of Victoria Road before turning right to reach Pioneer.

24. Shelley and Emley Moor

Summary: This is a longer, more arduous walk than most in this book. The circuit from Emley Moor to Shelley and back up the moorside uses paths and tracks of every description across the largely agricultural countryside, including a railway-side path and about two miles of minor road. Plenty of stiles, one or two of which might be found to be in a decrepit condition. Generally up and down but the ascent of the moor itself is steady rather then steep.

Length: 8 miles (12.8km). (full walk, including railway terminus).

Car Parking: Substantial roadside car parking area near the top of Emley Moor. Grid reference 222131.

Maps: Ordnance Survey Pathfinder 703, Wakefield South and area, 1:25,000. Ordnance Survey Landranger 110, Sheffield and Huddersfield, 1:50,000.

The Tea Shop

Spoilt for choice on arriving in Shelley – there are two admirable venues for tea. The Ice Cream Parlour at **Barkhouse Farm** is unusual. Ice cream is made here under the brand name of Dearne Lea and can be bought in large containers to take away or purchased for immediate consumption. Many flavours are available including toffee, banana, strawberry, the more unusual apple pie, and many others. All are of good quality and leave one wanting more! The building is a long room, the ice cream sales and food counter being near to the entrance and the tea room at the far end. The furnishings are good with dark wood tables and chairs. A miscellany of farm bric-a-brac, including a collection of milk bottles, is displayed round the room. Light cooked meals are served here as well as sandwiches, scones, homemade cakes, and even bowls of trifle; don't forget to sample at least one variety of ice cream.

Open: 10.30am to 5pm (last orders 4.30pm) every day all the year.Tel: 01484 602058

The alternative, and equally, attractive venue is the Coffee Shop at **The Pennine Garden Centre**, another café offering a good choice of food and drink. The surroundings are pleasant and the large windows offer long views of the countryside. The scones and cakes are good quality - the jam slice was scrumptious! - light meals, salads and sandwiches are available.

Open: 9.30am to 5pm every day but on Sunday the hours are from 10.30am to 4.30pm. Tel: 01484 607248

About the Area

Shelley is quite a large but generally unremarkable village situated a few miles to the south east of Huddersfield. To the east of the village the pleasantly rural landscape is dominated by Emley Moor or, perhaps more accurately, by the tall telecommunications mast on top of the moor. On this walk you can't really escape it. It should be said that Emley Moor is not a truly wild moor like those in the Pennines a few miles to the west of Huddersfield. It is more accurately a large upland area, with a summit at 264m (866ft.) and with agriculture creeping up the not so steep sides.

The Kirklees Light Railway uses four miles of the trackbed of a former Lancashire and Yorkshire Railway branch line. On this trackbed a 15-inch gauge line has been laid, with a main station and workshops at Clayton West. The line is steeply graded and includes

Kirklees Light Railway

a tunnel 511 yards in length. The attractive little steam locomotives include one which was built at Clayton West. The line is operated as a visitor attraction, every weekend throughout the year and every day from the Spring Bank Holiday to early September and other school holidays. At the station there is a visitor centre with souvenir shop and refreshments.

The Walk

Set off by turning right to follow the roadside, descending very gently and passing a small area of woodland. The village visible to the left is Flockton. After a road junction with Westfield Lane, pass a new house and then look carefully for a 'public footpath' sign on a stile, leading directly into the front garden of a house.

1. Go past the end of the house and over a stile in the boundary of the back garden. (There are, apparently, proposals for a minor diversion of this section of footpath).

   Pass through a smallholding, with Emley village in view to the left, and turn right, through a gate. Turn left and stay close to the side of a wall to descend to a decrepit stile. Go over and continue along the edge of a meadow to another stile. Pass through two more meadows before a solitary house is reached.

2. The path through the property is immediately to the left of a block of garages, with a ruinous farm to the left of the path.

   Cross a minor road to a 'public bridleway' sign and follow a stony lane, hedged on either side. Clayton West is in view ahead as the lane descends to pass Low House Farm; pheasants may be disturbed on this part of the walk. In 300 metres after the farm turn right at a gate/stile to take a footpath which keeps close to a wall on the left.

3. This area is Emley Park. Continue through a gate, now with a fence/hedge on the right, veering away to the left to a gate/stile, and cross a ditch.

   Go over another old metal stile in a few metres and ascend along the edge of a meadow. As a little valley is reached, ahead, turn right, along the field edge, for 40 metres then turn left to angle down the valley side on a clear path. Cross a little bridge and go up to a gate.

4. Go through and continue along the edge of a meadow with a wall on the left and a factory chimney ahead; Skelmanthorpe is in view to the left. Go through/over a gate/stile in the far-left corner and then another gate in 35 metres, giving access to a farm track. Turn right to walk to Park Gate, joining a minor public road. Turn left, downhill.

At the bottom turn right, between houses, initially on tarmac. The track soon becomes a pleasant lane, rising gently, part of 'Skelmanthorpe Village Trail'. Join another stony lane, turning left. Go across an unsurfaced road to a signposted stone stile, then up a meadow alongside a broken wall, to a stile at the top. Bear right to descend to a substantial footbridge over the railway line, here in a ravine-like cutting.

5. Cross and rise up the far side to a stile and keep to the left of a broken wall/hedge, then up a few steps to a public road. Turn right, downhill, on the roadside pavement. In about 200 metres, at the bottom of the dip, turn left at a 'public footpath' signpost, to follow a little path, initially under trees, then along the side of school playing fields.

6. Pass an ornamental pond in a house garden to the right.
At the next public road, turn right, then left in 40 metres at a 'public footpath' sign into a broad old lane between walls. To the right is the portal of the railway tunnel, seen only by making a small diversion from the track. The railway line emerges into a deep cutting. Regain the main track from any diversion and continue the descent to a minor road.

7. If you don't want to see the terminus of the railway, turn right at the road, Long Moor Lane, then right at a road junction to walk by the roadside up the hill to Shelley. Bear right as the main road through the village is reached, then left in 200 metres or so to the tea shop — the Ice Cream Parlour at Barkhouse Farm.

8. Alternatively, the **garden centre tea room** can be reached in another 100 metres by not turning left.
To see the turning point of the trains, follow the instructions in italic text: Cross Long Moor Lane and follow 'public footpath' signs through the property ahead, keeping to the right of the buildings and going over three stiles to continue by the lineside. There are more stiles before reaching a horse-riding establishment. Through a gate on the right, the end of the line, with turning loop, can be seen.

9. Continue by an access drive, cross a bridge over the main railway line (note the Lancashire and Yorkshire Railway notice), then find a minor footpath to the right of the houses ahead, and descend to the public road, over a stile.

10. *Turn right, go under a double railway bridge and walk up the road to Shelley village and the refreshments, as above.*
From the Ice Cream Parlour — turn left to walk uphill along the minor road.
From the garden centre — walk along to the church, go through the lychgate into the churchyard, exit by a small gate in the top right corner,

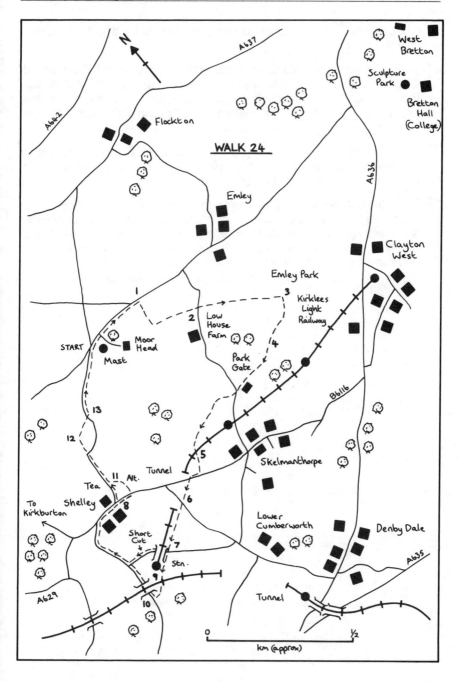

cross a small field, go over a stile, cross another field and go over another stile to reach the minor road.

11. There is a worn track along the grass on the left of the road. Pass a road junction and, as the road bends sharply to the right, turn left to a 'public footpath signpost. Go through the gate and stay close to the wall on the left up a rising meadow. At the wall angle at the top of the rise bear right towards Roydhouse hamlet and the communications mast.

12. There is a path over the grass just about visible, passing close to a lone ash tree. At the top go over a stile, into the hamlet, passing houses and bearing right to return to the public road.

13. Turn left and walk along the roadside, passing the Three Acres Inn. There are long views both to left and right and plenty of time to admire the sleek proportions of the mast, now close at hand. As the moor top is reached, pass a service reservoir, a road junction, a Certificated Location caravan site, a bridleway, another road junction and the buildings of the Communications Centre, before reaching the car park.

25. Overton and the Mining Museum

Summary: Surprisingly rural, this walk is based on the National Coal Mining Museum at the former Caphouse Colliery. There are no long ascents, no footpath difficulties and only two stiles. A good proportion of the route is in the attractive Stony Cliff woodland. Walking beside public roads totals about one third of a mile.

Length: 4¼ miles (7km)

Car Parking: At the museum, which is accessed from the A642 Huddersfield to Wakefield road. Note – the site barriers are closed at 5.15pm. Grid reference 253165.

Maps: Ordnance Survey Pathfinder 703, Wakefield South and area, 1;25,000. Ordnance Survey Landranger 110, Sheffield and Huddersfield, 1:50,000.

The Tea Shop

It is not necessary to pay to enter the Coal Mine Museum in order to take tea in 'The Miners' Pantry'; a very sensible system operates – just ask at reception. The café is, quite appropriately, something of a re-creation of a miners' canteen – Spartan but authentic; hygienic but characterful. Chintz and china would hardly be appropriate here so there are long Formica topped tables, with salt, pepper, and vinegar bottles much in evidence. Counter service with hot dishes available during the lunchtime period. Tea and coffee is served by the mug or cup. Authentic foods offered include chip butties and baked custards but there are more typically tea-time items such as the delicious chocolate shortbread.

Open: 10am to 5pm every day all the year except 24th, 25th, 26th December and 1st January. Tel: 01924 848806

About the Area

For many walkers this area between Huddersfield and Wakefield would hardly be first choice when planning a country walk. It is, however, surprisingly attractive countryside, with little evidence of either the formerly intensive coal mining activity or the proximity of large residential areas. One side of the valley is well wooded.

The focal point is obviously the former Caphouse Colliery which has been converted into a major visitor attraction, The National Coal Mining Museum for England, exhibiting a great array of mining activity and equipment, ancient and modern, including trips underground. The site also has picnic area, adventure playground and nature trail.

One of the many exhibits at the Mining Museum

The Walk

Leave the Mining Museum by the visitor vehicular entrance and turn left along the pavement beside the main road. Opposite the far end of the museum buildings turn right up a short minor road rising to connect with a more important road.

1. Turn left at the top along the roadside pavement. After passing the first house on the right, turn right into Smithy Lane, which loses its tarmac surface as an unexpected trig. point is reached. There are now long views over the flat countryside to the left, as far as the distant power stations at Ferrybridge and Eggborough. Emley Moor telecommunications mast is nearby, to the right. Continue to a meeting place of several tracks.

2. Turn left, then fork left in a few metres to walk downhill on a good, broad trail through agricultural country, with a tiny stream alongside on one sec-

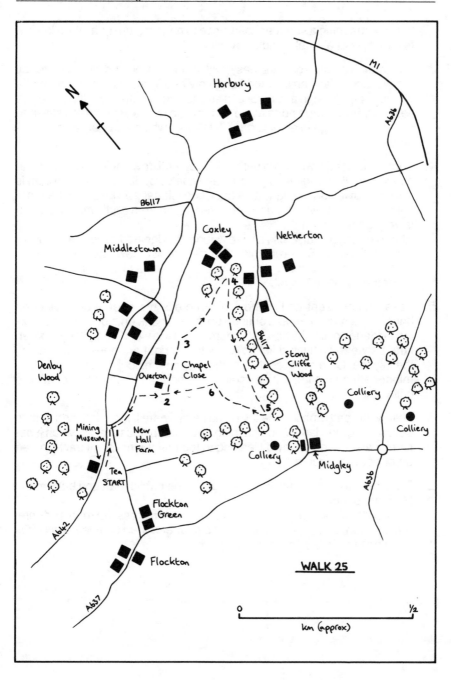

tion. On reaching a surfaced road close to houses, turn right, then left in a few metres at a 'public bridleway' sign.

3. The track is again broad and easy, with a little paving and with bramble by the wayside. Pass an isolated bungalow and immediately turn right at a 'public footpath' sign and go over a stile to take a path down the edge of a field, towards a large pond at the bottom. Go over a waymarked stile and cross a footbridge to enter Stony Cliff Wood, which is largely a nature reserve.

4. Turn right along a well worn path, a little up and down at first, but soon becoming level through the predominantly oak woodland. A little stream is never far away on the right. The track occasionally divides and there are minor side paths which must be ignored. Apart from a little mud the going is very good indeed.
After passing a seat, cross a wide wooden bridge and ascend sharply for a short distance. Stay with this main track which now has a stoned surface; silver birch trees are now plentiful. Reach a kissing gate, join another track and turn right.

5. Pass another seat and go downhill to cross the stream on a wooden bridge by a muddy area. Continue up the far bank on a good path showing evidence of use by horses. Emerge from the woodland, along a green lane between cultivated fields. Away to the right are houses built along the skyline. On a rising section of the green lane, look out carefully for a minor path on the left, which rises up the right-hand boundary of a large cultivated field.

6. Follow this path uphill to the top of the field, where it kinks left then right to become a green lane, soon passing an isolated house, after which it becomes a surfaced driveway leading to the major junction of tracks noted on our outward route.

2. From here turn left to retrace the route to the public road and back to the Mining Museum.
To avoid walking beside the main road, you can cross the road and enter the museum complex by a gate at the near end then bear left behind the buildings to circle back to the car park.

26. Yorkshire Sculpture Park, West Bretton

Summary: An easy walk, full of interest, on very good paths, largely through the spacious parkland of the sculpture park and the adjacent Bretton Country Park. A very small amount of ascent in the woodland to the south of Lower Lake. One stile; no other obstructions.

Length: 4¼ miles (7km)

Car Parking: Large pay and display car park by the visitor centre at the east end of the country park. Accessed directly from A637, Huddersfield to Barnsley road. Grid reference 295124

Maps: Ordnance Survey Pathfinder 703, Wakefield South and area, 1:25,000. Ordnance Survey Landranger 110, Sheffield and Huddersfield, 1:50,000.

The Tea Shop

The Bothy Café is right at the top of the park, so it is downhill all the way following tea. Having completed three-quarters of the distance one has certainly earned some refreshments. There are two small well-furnished tea rooms but the favourite place to sit is outdoors on the sheltered patio; from here there are long views across the park and countryside. Also, notice the interesting architecture of the nearby pavilion. Counter service with the usual range of food and drink.

Open: 11am to 5pm (closes 4pm in winter months) every day all the year but variable during the Christmas/New Year period. Tel: 01924 830043

About the Area

The Yorkshire Sculpture Park occupies more than 200 acres of the fine 18th century parkland of Bretton Hall, which is now used as a university college. The parkland is used for the spacious display of some of the best sculpture in Britain. Additionally, there are two indoor galleries, craft shop, bookshop and café. The permanent collection is enhanced by changing exhibitions, both indoors and outdoors, and an important collection of Henry Moore bronzes in the adjacent 100-acre Bretton Country Park. Admission to the parks is free. Other visitor facilities include an information centre and public conveniences at the sculpture park and a sculpture trail accessible for disabled people.

Sculpture at Bretton Park

The Walk

Go through the two multi-waymarked small gates by the car park visitor centre. Follow the tarmac path into the open parkland, forking left by a seat to take a minor track, descending slightly, soon reaching the first of the many Henry Moore sculptures which grace this parkland. Turn left through an old iron gate to cross an attractive 18th century bridge and then the dam at the bottom end of Lower Lake.

1. Pass a gate leading to a conservation study area, then go left up steep steps through woodland, largely silver birch. The well-used path winds among the trees. Go down a few steps and then up to two stiles. Take that on the right to follow the red trail

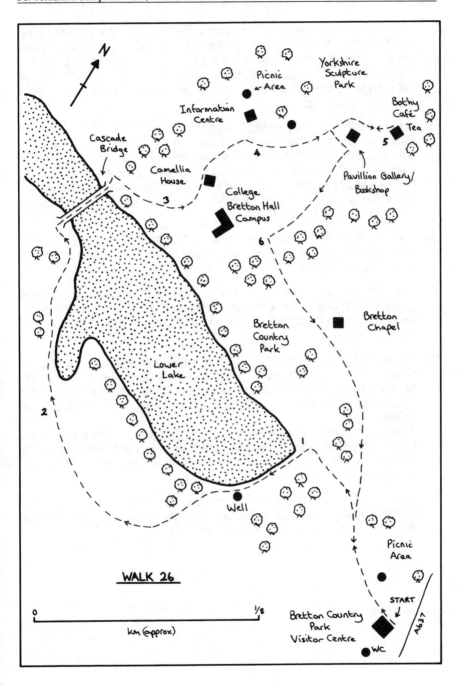

N

Yorkshire
Sculpture
Park

Picnic
Area

Information
Centre

Bothy
Café
Tea

Cascade
Bridge

5

4

Pavillion Gallery/
Bookshop

Camellia
House

3

College
Bretton Hall
Campus

6

Bretton
Chapel

Bretton
Country
Park

Lower
Lake

2

1

Well

Picnic
Area

WALK 26

START

A637

0   ⅛

km (approx)

Bretton Country
Park
Visitor Centre

WC

Continue by bearing right, downhill, along a wide, stony, path, soon reaching open hillside. Below, on the right, is what could be a long disused (railway?) cutting. Pass a red marker post; the path here becomes rougher but is still perfectly adequate as it joins a track which could be an old railway trackbed. Leave the red marked path by bearing to the right along this wide track.

2. Bretton Hall is in view, ahead through the trees. Bear left, join another track and turn right through an old iron gate. A broad, stony, track descends towards the lake. Cross Cascade Bridge, between the two lakes, then bear right to enter the Sculpture Park at a gate/stile/kissing gate. Follow a wide easy track through the sculpture-adorned parkland. As the track bends to the right, before passing the Hall, turn left over grass, a broad, tree-dotted, sward.

3. There is no path but keep the stone built Camellia House well to your right. Continue along a path rising to pass close to modern college buildings to reach the extensive car parking area by the main visitor centre.

4. From this centre head for the tea shop at the Bothy by going uphill, over grass, aiming well to the right of the vehicle access drive. Pass the modernistic Pavilion building; the Bothy is at the top of the large enclosed area.

5. Leave the Bothy, return to the Pavilion, turn left and left again to reach a broad terrace usually used for temporary exhibitions. Go down the terrace steps and angle to the left over grass to pass a lily pond on your right. Keep well to the left to stay above a roadway, which has a 'private' notice.
   Keep close to a narrow belt of woodland on the left to descend past a college building and join a surfaced roadway. Turn left and then, in 20 metres, turn left again between old stone pillars and over a cattle grid to reach a gate.

6. Follow an excellent grass track across the country park, leading directly to the car park, with as many diversions to right and left as you wish to see the Henry Moore sculpture at close quarters.

27. Cannon Hall and High Hoyland

Summary: Forget the proximity of Barnsley, Wakefield and the M1. This is a real country walk, combining the fine parkland of Cannon Hall with rolling agricultural countryside and the extensive woodland of Cawthorne Park and Deffer Wood. There is great variety in the footpaths, some clear and some not so clear, and some mud is likely. Prolonged but steady ascent to High Hoyland. Half a mile is along a minor road and there are ten stiles in total.

Length: 5 miles (8km)

Car Parking: Large pay and display car park, with public conveniences, close to Cannon Hall. Grid reference 272080.

Maps: Ordnance Survey Pathfinder 715, Barnsley and Penistone, 1:25,000 (most of walk). Ordnance Survey Pathfinder 703, Wakefield South and area, 1:25,000 (a small portion at High Hoyland). Ordnance Survey Landranger 110, Sheffield and Huddersfield, 1:50,000

The Tea Shop

Having looked at three possibilities for tea we decided to go to the café at The Garden Centre – an admirable venue with the choice of the light, bright, well-furnished little café or the sheltered patio amongst the pots and plants. Well displayed food – particularly marvellous vanilla slices – choice of tea, coffee, cold drinks, and ice creams. Very definitely a 'feel good' tea shop right at the end of the walk and the car park is just across the road!

Open: 10am to 4.30pm (closes at 4pm in the winter months) every day all the year except Christmas Day, Boxing Day, and New Year's Day. Tel: 01226 790785

About the Area

There is a considerable area of attractive countryside situated between Huddersfield and Barnsley, well wooded and with the parkland of Cannon Hall as a highlight. The Hall was the home of the Spencer Stanhope family for 200 years and, with the parkland, is now in the care of Barnsley Metropolitan District Council. The

Council operates the estate as a considerable visitor attraction, open to the public daily (except Mondays other than Bank Holidays) from the beginning of April to the end of October. Winter opening is more restricted – tel. 01226 790270 for details. The house contains a museum with collections of pottery, furniture and paintings, including two galleries with glass and Moorcroft pottery collections. Local military history is also featured. There is a museum shop and refreshments. Outside, a walled garden of the 1760s is a particular attraction.

The small visitor centre at the car park opens only at weekends during the high season, with extra opening during the school summer holidays.

High Hoyland is an unpretentious village with a pretty inn and long views to the south, as far as the Derbyshire hills on a clear day.

Very close to the line of this walk, Cawthorne is an attractive village with a fair amount of visitor interest. This includies a disused drinking fountain, a big stone cross and the small Victoria Jubilee Museum, run by volunteers, open during the afternoon at weekends and Bank Holiday Mondays, from Palm Sunday until the end of October. The parish church is much renovated, with a 15th century tower, a cross in the churchyard with Saxon carving and the head of another Saxon cross built into the church wall.

The Walk

Leave the car park and turn left along the adjacent road, crossing an elegant little bridge over a stream. In a few metres, turn left through an old iron kissing gate.

1. There is no path, but go straight ahead over close cropped grass, with the long but narrow lake close on the left. There are some good specimens of oak trees and plenty of noisy geese by the lake.

    In less than half a mile reach a surfaced track which crosses the lake on a bridge to the left. Ignore the bridge, turning right towards a gate. Immediately before the gate turn left along a footpath with a hedge on the right. In 100 metres go round the end of a gate; waymarks here include the Barnsley Boundary Walk. Go through a little woodland, along the edge of a small field, then pass a cricket field to reach a three-way signpost close to the vehicular entrance to the cricket club.

2. Turn left to follow 'Bridleway, Kexbrough 1.5 miles'. Go through a gate and cross a stream on a footbridge by a ford to reach an unsurfaced lane.

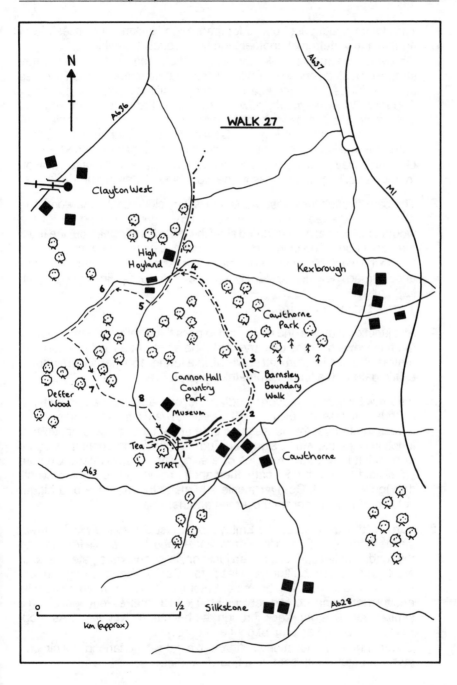

Turn left at a signpost ' public footpath High Hoyland, 1.5 miles'. Fork right in a few metres at another sign 'Kexbrough 1.3 miles'

Go over a waymarked stile and along a field edge path. Cross a tiny stream on a plank bridge to a stile with several waymarks. Go left to cross another, bigger, watercourse on a bridge, still following the Barnsley Boundary Walk waymark, now very familiar. From here, our route is straight across a large meadow, aiming for a gate on the far side. The path is faintly visible on the grass. Continue through/over the waymarked gate/stile and keep the same line, rising beside a hawthorn hedge.

Go over a waymarked stile, cross a ditch on a plank bridge and carry on to another stile giving access to the woodland of Cawthorne Park.

3. The path through the dense woodland is very clear. Leave the woodland at a stile and keep close to the wall on the right, still rising. Enter the woodland again at a waymarked stile; the route is very clear, but the track may be muddy. The diversified woodland has plenty of beech.

Leave the wood by a low wall to follow a grass path to a Water Company access road, now rising, steeply at the end, towards High Hoyland, village, above.

Turn left at the public road.

4. At a junction stay with the main road to pass the Cherry Tree Inn, sharing the fine views over the countryside to the south. At a road junction 150 metres after the inn, turn left downhill. In a further 150 metres turn right at a little gate with a 'public footpath' signpost.

5. A narrow track rises through woodland, following yellow marker posts. At a house access drive turn right, uphill, towards more houses. Pass across the front of the houses to a gate at the far end and proceed to a junction of paths, with a signpost. Turn right to reach another junction, turning left here at the remains of a stile, with faint waymark. Cross a small field on a well worn path, then another field and continue downhill through woodland. Go over a stile and along the top edge of a bigger field, to reach a minor road over yet another stile.

6. Turn left along the road. The Emley Moor mast is, inevitably in this area, visible to the right. Pass a large farm and, in about half a mile from joining the road, turn left opposite a road junction, through/over a gate/stile situated just before buildings. Head for Deffer Wood along an old stone-walled lane, rich in bramble. Enter the wood at a waymarked stile and turn left along a broad vehicular track. In 20 metres fork right along a similar, very straight, track through the beech-rich woodland. As progress is made, the amount of conifer increases.

Go straight on at a junction and through a gate at the far end to a circular stone structure, with seat, at a fine viewpoint.

Viewing station at Deffer Wood

7. Go through another gate, bearing left to descend through more wood-land, now on a narrow path. Emerge into more open country, with a curi-ous battlemented structure on the left.

Cross over a minor road and continue along a roadway into the Cannon Hall Estate.

8. Join a wider, surfaced road; to the left is the visitor complex including the Open Farm and the Hall, with museum. To the right the road descends di-rectly to the car park. The recommended tea shop is at the garden centre on the far side of the public road.

Tea Shop Walks – Spreading everywhere!

The Sigma Leisure Tea Shop Walks series already includes:

**Cheshire – Chilterns – Clwydian Hills & Welsh Borderlands
Cotswolds – Lake District, Volumes 1 & 2 – Lancashire
Leicestershire & Rutland – Lleyn and Anglesey – North Devon
Peak District – Shropshire – Snowdonia – South Devon
Staffordshire – Surrey & Sussex – Warwickshire – Yorkshire Dales**

Each book costs £6.95 and contains an average of 25 excellent walks: far better value than any other competitor!

Also of interest:

WEST YORKS WALKS: KIRKLEES
Martin Brewis
These 26 walks are all circular, range from 3 to 7 miles, and will help you discover the diverse beauty of the area. From walks centred on the secluded towns and villages in the Holme, Colne and Spen valleys to spectacular panoramic views from high ridges, there's a walk to grab everyone's imagination.   £6.95

WEST YORKS WALKS: CALDERDALE & BRADFORD
Martin Brewis
26 circular walks which explore the dramatic landscape of Calderdale and Bradford. Surprisingly this includes rolling Pennine moorland, secluded dales, deans and cloughs and farming villages around Todmorden, Sowerby and Hebden Bridge, Haworth and Ilkley. Detailed routes are complemented by 'points of interest' for the inquisitive walker.   £6.95

In case of difficulty, or for a free catalogue, please contact:
**SIGMA LEISURE,
1 SOUTH OAK LANE, WILMSLOW, CHESHIRE
SK9 6AR.**
Phone: 01625-531035
Fax: 01625-536800.
E-mail: info@sigmapress.co.uk
Web site: http//www.sigmapress.co.uk

VISA and MASTERCARD orders welcome.